# it's just a dinner party

# it's just a dinner party

the modern approach to entertaining with style and ease

## Ron and Julie Malloy

CAPITAL
BOOKS, INC.
Sterling, Virginia

**Capital Books, Inc.
Sterling, Virginia**

Capital Books, Inc.
P.O. Box 605
Herndon, Virginia  20172-0605

Photographs © 2001 by Steve Landis. All rights reserved.

**Library of Congress Cataloging-in-Publication Data**

Malloy, Ron.
    It's just a dinner party / Ron and Julie Malloy. --1st ed.
        p. cm.
    ISBN 1-892123-64-9
     1. Entertaining. I. Malloy, Julie. II. Title.

 TX731 .M353 2001
 642'.4--dc21                                                    2001037231

Printed in the United States of America on acid-free paper that meets the
American National Standards Institute Z39-48 Standard.

First Edition

10 9 8 7 6 5 4 3 2 1

We dedicate this book to our parents.

# contents

# welcome

We work hard, play as much as we can, strive to find balance between life and work, and aspire to live good, successful lives. In short, we're probably a lot like you.

Even though it often seems as if there isn't a spare second in each day to unwind, let alone plan for something as "frivolous" as a dinner party, the fact is: we love to entertain, and we do it all the time.

Unfortunately, many of our peers think entertaining is a time-consuming, arts and crafts–driven contest. And we can't blame them. From the magazines and books out there, it certainly seems as if entertaining "correctly" requires hand-stenciling place cards and making your own goat cheese!

But while merging the "domestic arts" with entertaining might be ideal for some people (people with a lot of free time)—it isn't necessary.

If you think you might enjoy entertaining but find that you're too busy to make doilies and that you lack the time (and the space) to raise chickens—then this book is for you. We want you to know that entertaining does not require the use of a hot glue gun, and it isn't some competition in which only housewives can participate.

It is our goal to illustrate that entertaining shouldn't be intimidating, and that it can be a tremendous source of joy.

You see, early on in our relationship we discovered something priceless: that entertaining together is fun and enormously rewarding. One of us cooks, the other sets everything up, and we clean the whole mess up as a team. Entertaining gives us time together, the opportunity to establish friendships with other people together, to learn things together, and to experience a wide range of emotions together (joy, anxiety, pressure and relief, to name a few). It can be that way for every couple.

Despite the well-publicized image of entertaining as a fussy woman's task, the truth is, the real beauty of entertaining isn't found in the décor, or the food or the flower arrangements. The beauty in entertaining resides in the life that emerges when several unique people get together. Sure, entertaining can include moments of near perfection and artistry, just as it almost always includes awkward moments, mistakes and embarrassment. But the most gorgeous aspect of any event is its humanity.

And entertaining is easy! Here's what you won't find in this book: arts and crafts instructions, elaborate baking recipes, anything that requires pinking shears or ribbon. Why won't you find these things here? Because they're unnecessary fluff. The things you might read about in other entertaining guides —"rules," "standards," things considered "good"—are absolutely not important.

*Any fool can make a rule, and any fool will mind it.*

Henry David Thoreau

What you will find in this book is an abundance of real-life, simple advice and hints that we've found helpful in our years of entertaining together. We share basics with you, like:

- Buy extra ice.
- Hot rooms make people sleepy.
- Your guests are more valuable than your crystal.

Let us be the first to tell you that the only important element in every party is the guests (and as a host, you are your own guest—please, never forget that). Not the monogrammed tea towels, not the fancy trivets, not the elaborate dessert: the guests.

Whether you're the Queen Mum or a working mom, your guests don't come to your party to compete with or be impressed by you. And they certainly don't come over to gawk at your garden or the marble tile in your new bathroom. They simply come to be with you.

We're not only going to show you how to plan and prepare for a party—which we do, with a twist. We're going to show you how to truly welcome your guests. We'll show you how to treat them and yourself well, with honor and respect. In short, we're going to teach you (or just remind you) how to be a gracious host.

We firmly believe that it is in grace—not taste—that true style is found.

*Taste: a quality possessed by persons without originality or moral courage.*

George Bernard Shaw

Friends, it's time to get real. Entertaining can mean ordering in Chinese food for four or a three hundred person fundraiser—and if you have the proper perspective, it should never be terribly hard.

You should forget about the quest for someone else's unattainable standards of perfection and follow us. We're going to show you the modern way to entertain with style and grace. And we'll show you how to have a great time doing it.

So drop the hot glue gun and step away from that stenciling kit. Entertaining isn't a contest and it shouldn't be intimidating . . . after all, it's just a dinner party.

To successfully learn from this book, all you need to do is turn the page and read . . . and then practice. Great hosts aren't born—they're made. Be patient with yourself and have fun learning. The most important thing to remember is to be true to yourself and kind to your guests.

*Kindness is always fashionable.*

Amelia E. Burr

We're here if you need us. Enjoy!

# acknowledgments

We would like to thank our parents for their love and constant support, and for being great teachers in the art of living a full, happy life. We'd also like to thank Alison, Jeff and Susy, for never asking us to be anyone but ourselves, and Christian and Alexander, just for being our Godchildren. Gatsby and Garbo: happiness truly is a warm puppy.

A very special thank you to our grandparents, for their stories, wisdom and laughter, all of which is priceless even if only a memory. And to all of our relatives and every one of our friends: thank you for being inspirational, supportive and always interesting.

Thank you Steve Landis, for your talent, patience, sense of humor, and all of the terrific photographs. Special thanks to all our "models" for being so fabulous, and to the staff at the Stamford Yacht Club for so kindly rolling with us. To everyone at Capital Books, we are extraordinarily grateful for this opportunity and appreciate your expert assistance. Thank you.

Importantly, we would like to thank all of the guests who have graced our parties with their presence. You have enriched our lives and contributed to many wonderful memories.

And thank all of you for reading this book.

# foundation

**T**he person who tries to live alone will not succeed as a human being.

His heart withers if it does not answer another heart.

His mind shrinks away as he hears only the echoes of his own thoughts and finds no inspiration.

Pearl S. Buck

# guest-centric

The foundation of all social entertaining is the guests. After all, it wouldn't be a party without them, would it?

We call our approach "guest-centric" entertaining. No, this isn't some strange, new-age, candle-and-incense ritual. Guest-centric entertaining means that as a host, you should be focusing on your guests' comfort and happiness throughout the entire process.

When you practice guest-centric entertaining, you keep your guests in mind from the first planning stages until the last one of them goes home (or to bed), and you remember the following:

- Your guests are the most important element of your party.
- Your guest's comfort and happiness does not involve being impressed.
- You are your most important guest.

*True politeness consists in being easy on one's self,*
*and in making everyone about one as easy as one can.*

Alexander Pope

Leonard Bernstein, reflecting on an evening he spent at the Kennedy White House, said:

> You were served very good drinks first. . . . There were ashtrays everywhere just inviting you to poison yourself with cigarettes. . . . The moment comes for you to greet the President and the First Lady. . . . Who couldn't be more charming if they tried, who make you feel utterly welcome, even with a huge gathering. . . . The food is marvelous, the wines are delicious, there are cigarettes on the table, people are laughing, laughing out loud, telling stories, jokes, enjoying themselves, glad to be there. . . . You know, I've never seen so many happy artists in my life. It was a joy to watch it.
>
> *In the Kennedy Style: Magical Evenings in the Kennedy White House*

Letitia Baldridge

Interestingly, what he remembered is how happy the guests were made to be; this is the result of the guest-centric approach. He didn't mention the china, the centerpieces or the linens; he remembered extremely happy guests.

When you take a guest-centric approach to entertaining, you can't help but provide a warm, welcoming event that will be remembered fondly.

Keep in mind, however, that you are your own guest. Your guests need you to have a good time with them. If you've ever been to a party where the host is stressed out, upset or never leaves the kitchen, you know what we mean. It can be very distracting or worrisome. This is why the host's happiness is crucial to guest-centric entertaining.

You are your own guest. Your happiness is paramount to your guests' enjoyment.

- Honor yourself and your own personal style.
- Don't do anything that makes you uncomfortable.
- Don't take on anything too time-consuming.
- Don't stretch yourself too far financially.

*Joy is a net of love by which you can catch souls.*

Mother Teresa

# establishing
# the event

Getting started is often the hardest part. To begin, you need to make some very basic decisions that essentially outline your party and define it. Just like any project (think of a proposal for work or a business trip itinerary), it is helpful to know what you are doing and why before you start.

First, establish the overall concept. Then imagine your guests at your party—having a fantastic time.

- Who are they?
- What are they doing?
- Where are they?
- Why are they there?
- When is it?

These are the five journalistic "Ws" most of us know: who, what, where, why and when. The reason journalists use them is because once they've answered the five Ws, they've got the bones of a story. The same applies for entertaining: once you've answered the five Ws, you've created the outline for a party.

who
- do you want to entertain?
- do you need to entertain?
  - what do they like?
    - are they celebrating?

what
- type of party suits them?
  - formal dinner
  - casual dinner
  - cocktails
  - big, festive event
  - a theme

where
- would guests like to be?
  - indoors
  - outside
  - a unique location
- can they travel to?
- is best this time of year?

why
- are you having the party?
    - you want to
    - work-related
    - it's family
    - to celebrate an occasion
    - a holiday
    - an event

when
- is best for the guests?
    - do they have children?
    - are they elderly?
- is the best time at location?
    - beauty
    - light
    - comfort

# invitations

Once you establish your party, the next step is inviting your guests. The invitation will become the outline for your planning and will set the stage for the event. We don't like to spend too much time on one topic, but lots of people seem to be intimidated by invitations, and even more people get them wrong. All you really have to remember is to give your guests enough time, give them a little inspiration to come, and give them enough information that it won't be hard for them to come.

## timing

Luckily, if you use your head and know your guests (applying the guest-centric approach), you'll fall within the rules of etiquette on timing naturally. Know your guests and what their lives are like. Do they have kids? Are you inviting the kids or will they need a sitter? Is anyone elderly or unable to drive in the dark? Accommodate all of your invitees. That said, you can always fall back on the "rules," which are:

- Three to six weeks for a formal dinner
- A few days to three weeks for informal dinners, lunches or teas
- Two to four weeks for a cocktail party

You're Invited
Julie and Ron Malloy's Sixth Annual "Blues Party"
Saturday May 14
6:00 p.m.- cocktails and hors d'oeuvres
Dinner and dancing to follow
Featuring live Blues 'til midnight
111 Their Street
Their City,CT 12345
Map and directions enclosed

come casual- but wear blue

Please respond by May 7
203.555.1111

Mr. and Mrs. Joe Smith
1234 Any Street
Any City, State 12345

- Two to six weeks for a holiday dinner
- Last-minute invitations, written or called, are fine only for very casual get-togethers or family

Avoid telephone and email invitations. They are unreliable and better suited for spontaneous, informal parties.

# information

You wouldn't know it from what you see in other books or magazines, but the most important element in an invitation is the information. Not the fluff, glitter, bows, paper quality or typeface. The information.

Luckily, you already know the basics:

- Who the party is for
- What type of party it is—and what type of food will be served
- Where it is
- Why you are having the party
- When the party is

Include this information in your invitation.  Then add:

- Who you are and how to reach you
- An RSVP requirement and instructions
- A map or written directions to the event location
- Other pertinent information (attire, gift acceptance, etc.)

Remember, your guests should not have to pull a Sherlock Holmes to figure out whether to bring a gift, what to wear, where you live, or how to RSVP. It shouldn't be hard to attend a party. Give them the information. Also, try to avoid cutesy terms or vague instructions. "Festive Attire" could lead to guests arriving in thong bikinis, body glitter and feather headdresses. Be warned (and be more specific).

# reality check

### envelopes

While they seem mundane, envelopes can be very helpful. In fact, they can eliminate a lot of confusion.

If children are invited, for example, add "and family" to the recipient line; if a date should come, add "and guest," and so on. Or, if you only want a husband and wife to come, simply address the envelope to "Mr. and Mrs. John Smith."

Also: make sure they're mailable.

Don't mail a folded over, stapled piece of paper. They get crumpled, eaten, and generally lost by the postal service. If it's oversized or undersized, have it weighed and checked by a postal worker. For larger mailings, it is smart to find out how much postage will cost before buying the invitations; we can't tell you how often we've heard people complain about wedding invitations costing twice or triple what they'd expected to spend on postage.

## inspiration

While we don't encourage spending a preponderance of free time making your invitations, the appearance of your invitations is important for two reasons.

- Invitations set the tone of your party.
- Invitations should be "inviting."

Common sense rules here. If you want your guests to come in black tie, be sure your invitation reflects that kind of quality and effort. If you want your guests to come and "let it all hang out," your invitation should portray this. You don't need to go overboard, but remember: an invitation is a written way of asking people to do you the favor of attending your party. Ask nicely.

# planning

You've already done the hardest part, which is making decisions and committing yourself by creating and (possibly) mailing out invitations. Now it's time to plan. Try to keep a guest-centric approach while planning, and be true to yourself. Remember that for your guests to be happy, you need to be happy—and that's what matters.

Don't bow to "good taste" or buckle under peer pressure. When you plan your party, think of the following quotation, from someone who knew more about style and creativity than anyone barking rules about taste to you today (including us):

*Taste is the enemy of creativeness.*

Pablo Picasso

Of course, while you want to be as unrestrained as possible in making yourself and your guests happy, you have to be realistic. The first step in planning, then, is taking a realistic look at the big picture. Review your overall concept and assess it realistically. Sushi for 50? An elegant dinner for 30? Sure, these parties sound lovely, but sushi is highly labor intensive, and you'd need a very large dining room to seat 30 guests. Look at the party you want to have, and make sure it is the party you *can* have. And if your plan needs a little adjusting, don't worry. There are many ways to adapt.

At our first annual Cinco de Mayo party, we decided to serve margaritas and fajitas for 150 guests—with no help. Both margaritas and fajitas need a ton of preparation and last-second labor. Luckily, we had a lot of chips and salsa, and our guests really enjoyed our margaritas! So they didn't notice (or care) that dinner didn't get served until nearly 10:00 P.M. This was a good learning experience for us. We learned to be more realistic.

# location, location

First, think about where you want to have the party. Is there enough space for the number of guests you want? Does the space lend itself well to the party you want to have? Can you use the space (is it available)?

First and foremost, don't limit your parties to the size of your home. Even if you have a closet-sized apartment, you can have a huge party. All you have to do is go elsewhere.

Try:

- Local restaurants
- Bars
- Clubs and hotels
- Museums
- Theaters
- Art galleries and museums
- Horse races
- Beaches
- Boats
- Parks

# need some **help**?

Hiring help can be one of the best ways to truly provide a guest-centric experience for you and your guests. It isn't an admission of incompetence—and it doesn't have to be expensive.

## reality check

### staffing requirements

Most caterers will calculate this for you. Use this list if you're hiring your own help. These vary for event—type of food and manner served, and so on—the more complicated, the more staff you'll need.

### cocktail/finger food parties

- 1 waiter per 20 guests
- 1 bartender for 100 guests
- 2 bartenders per 100 guests if drinks are mixed

### dinner parties

- 1 waiter per 10 guests (food service)
- 1 waiter per 20 guests (drink service)
- Bar staffing is the same as for cocktail parties
- 1 cook per 50 guests for finger food
- 1 cook per 20 guests for fork food (depends on food)

Remember that when you enjoy the party, your guests enjoy the party. Nobody wants a host they never see because he spends all night in the kitchen.

Hiring help can be wonderful and it doesn't have to be expensive. While professional caterers, chefs, staff and bartenders will do everything from preparation to cleanup, many caterers will staff your parties even if you don't use their catering services.

Consider hiring neighborhood kids or local college students to work your parties. They are more than capable, and they are usually excited to get the work. Ask them to wear simple black pants and shoes and a white shirt, with their hair pulled back, and you'll never know the difference between them and a professional staff (except the cost).

# rentals

Don't let the contents of your china cabinet dictate the size of your party. You can rent an amazing array of entertaining equipment.

- Dishes
- Glassware
- Flatware
- Chairs

- Tables
- Linens
- Tents
- Fans
- Heaters
- Equipment
- Grills
- Candlesticks

In addition, most rental companies can advise you on quantities per guest for all of their equipment. This comes in handy when figuring out numbers of tables and your space.

Also, health codes require rental companies wash all of the dishes, flatware and glassware they rent to you. So you don't need to wash anything—just rinse and crate it up—and they do the scrubbing.

## tunes

Music can be the backbone of a great party—or it can be flat-out annoying. So before booking that "rocking blues band" you saw (or think you saw) last weekend after your third martini, ask yourself:

- What will it add to this particular party—will it enhance the mood?
- Do you have the space—for a band, a dance floor, guests, food and a bar?
- Do your guests even like this type of music?
- Do your guests like to dance, or are most of them conversationalists?

## eight things to remember
### about live music

1 Don't sequester the musicians; they need to be central to the party.
2 If you want a dance floor, put it near the band and in a central location.
3 Tape down any electrical cords so that nobody trips on them.
4 Be sure the music never gets so loud that it kills conversation.
5 Schedule the music appropriately (i.e., softer music during the meal).
6 If you want to save money, hire the band directly, without a talent agency.
7 Discuss attire ahead of time (or don't complain when they come in leather).
8 Remember that it's customary to feed the band, and that they will take breaks.

Bear in mind, too, that live music can be loud. Remember your neighborhood. When we have a band, we indicate "live music" in the invitation—and invite everyone in the surrounding area.

20

# and now for the **little** things

Once you establish the "big picture" of your event, move on to focus on the details—the little things (that count). Please remember that it is entirely possible to get bogged down in unnecessary detail and extravagance (the little things that don't count). Try not to. You will be surprised by what your guests don't notice.

*Our life is frittered away by detail. Simplicity! Simplicity! Simplicity!*

Henry David Thoreau

The following are the three essential elements of a party, aside from the guests and the host. Everything else is fluff.

- Food
- Drink
- Space

# food

## simple

At home, simple is better. Most likely, you aren't a professional chef. (If you are, we apologize—and send us your favorite recipes, would you please?) Your food is probably not going to surpass the food your guests can get in a good restaurant. (Don't worry—your guests already know this. So should you.) Many attempts at "spectacular" food at home end up being spectacularly scary.

*Simplicity is the glory of expression.*

Walt Whitman

- Stick with natural, simple foods.
- Follow classic, time-tested recipes and menus.
- Stick with recipes within your skill level (and be honest with yourself).
- Read the time estimates on each recipe (and add 30 minutes).
- Master a few dishes and serve them regularly.
- In a pinch, let someone else do the cooking for you.

We have provided a few recipes in "elements," along with a list of our all-time favorite cookbooks. Most of these cookbooks include menus and suggestions on compatible dishes.

# provide

Part of being a caring host is providing for your guests. Provide a diverse enough menu to compensate for most food issues (preferences, allergies). While you may not know every food issue your guests have, extra side dishes and salads and an abundance of breads and starches ensure that none of your guests will leave the table hungry.

A meal is a celebration. Make sure everyone can participate.

# get **fat**

Don't submit your guests to your diet. They're not on it. Use salt, butter, oils, sugar and other non-dietetic ingredients. These ingredients make everything taste better.

Serve an appealing dessert. While nothing has to be fancy, it should be good. There is nothing better than some good old chocolate chip cookies and a glass of milk, so long as they're not "sugar free" and the milk is whole.

# reality check

**"to buffet or not to buffet?"— it could have been Hamlet's question . . .**

**To know, ask yourself:**

- Will your guests be comfortable?
- Can they all handle balancing a plate?
- Does a buffet suit the event and the location?

**If you decide to serve food buffet style:**

- Walk the buffet table to ensure easy flow.
- Make the starting point obvious.
- Edit any décor that gets in the way.
- Place coordinating foods by one another.

- Put plates, utensils in a logical place.
- Put serving utensils near each platter.
- Provide all necessary utensils and napkins.
- Don't tie utensils in napkins with ribbon—less dexterous guests can't untie them.
- Set buffets up for each course if possible.
- Clean up the buffet periodically.
- Restock food items consistently.

The elaborately decorated buffet tables you see in magazines are works of art— they don't have to feed 30 hungry people. Be realistic.

# luck

While we don't recommend hosting "pot luck" meals unless you're entertaining close family or a large group in a special situation (you're making your guests work, after all), if you do choose to go "pot luck," use a lot of logic and give a little direction.

It seems easy enough, asking your guests to bring a dish; you ask, they bring, you set it out, and everyone eats. Then the party starts, and people arrive, proudly carrying their dishes. And your buffet becomes a gastronomic battlefield.

With Aunt Mimi's famous sauerkraut alongside Priscilla's pepperoni pizza and Marge's marshmallow magic taking the rear, you'll boost Alka Seltzer sales, surely, but you won't be doing your guests or yourself any favors. The remedy?

Simply plan your menu ahead of time and suggest a dish for each guest to bring or a food category for them to work within. While you don't need to supply actual recipes, a theme adds clarification and reduces confusion. Most guests will know not to bring sushi to a Mexican-theme event.

You can prepare the main course and have your guests bring side dishes and so forth, which eliminates confusion. If you can, delegate in a guest-centric way. If one guest loves to cook, ask him to bring a nice side dish. If another guest dislikes cooking, ask her to bring chips.

Also, for non-"pot luck" events for which certain guests insist on bringing dishes, you are well within your right as a host to (politely) refuse their help or to specify what dish you would like them to bring.

# take **out**

If you don't know the difference between a pot and a pan, or if the thought of cooking is distasteful, then don't cook—and remember the two golden words of modern menu planning . . . take out.

This isn't 1953. You're not being judged on your scratch cake.

We're all busy. And if you don't already know, there is a lot of good food out there waiting to be bought and gussied up for your guests. If your guests ask how you made it, be honest and proud.

- Take out provides great food for your guests.
- Take out frees you up to have a better time.
- It's like bringing in a ringer when your team hasn't won a game all season.

Check your local phone book or call your favorite restaurants for local ideas. Most restaurants cater events, big or small, but they won't necessarily provide service staff. If you order in, simply take the food that gets delivered (or picked up) and put it in your own serving dishes.

There are online shops that deliver fantastic hors d'oeuvres or desserts (and even main courses). Of course, you need to think this through ahead of time (whereas local places can be relied upon close to the last minute). In "elements," we've provided you with a great list of online and over-the-phone resources.

# drinks

Drinks can be very important. Depending on your guests and the party you decide to throw, they can be central (cocktail party, margarita party). Even when they're not the focus of the party, they should at least complement the food and please and accommodate your guests.

When choosing beverages for your party, don't forget to provide plenty of nonalcoholic beverages for those who don't indulge.

Your guests should never be empty-handed (unless they want to be). The process of holding something in one's hand and the act of drinking seems to put people at ease. Provide a means for your guests to always have a drink when they want one. Don't make them sound like Oliver Twist, having to ask, "May I have some more, Sir?"

For small parties, you can probably serve guests yourself. The number of guests that proves too many for you to do this properly depends on you, but you may not want to handle more than eight guests yourself. Above eight guests, consider hiring help or providing a self-service bar. If you decide upon a self-service bar, check "elements" for helpful lists and tips.

Whatever you decide, like your second-grade teacher probably told you when you came to class with gum or candy, "You should have enough for everybody." Have enough of every type of drink you're serving, for all of your guests, for the whole party.

# **cool** as ice

The rule of thumb on ice is one pound per person—more on a very hot day. We've never witnessed too much ice putting a damper on an event, but we have seen what not enough ice can do.

# reality check

## bar basics

The following quantities are general. Know your guests. Keep in mind the time of day and weather, and don't forget about your Uncle who guzzles Wild Turkey.

### quantities

One bottle of wine = four 6 oz glasses
One bottle of Champagne = 6 flutes
One liter of hard liquor = twenty-two
   1.5 oz drinks
One case of wine = 12 bottles
One case of beer = 24 bottles/cans

## calculations for a 2-hour cocktail party:

1 liter hard liquor for every 10 drinkers
1 bottle for every 2 guests who drink wine
1 bottle of Champagne for every 2 guests who drink it
4 bottles of beer for every beer drinker

*The New American Bartender's Guide* says it best:

*A lukewarm drink makes a lukewarm guest.*

Be generous. Most liquor stores will accept unopened bottles for return (check first). Extra ice melts.

> The first time we hosted the annual family Fourth of July party, we underestimated how the heat would directly affect the thirstiness of our guests. Needless to say, we ran out of beer and had to ask our cousin John to drive to the nearest open liquor store, which was a state away (New York) and a half-hour drive in each direction. Since then, we do two things every year: check the extended weather forecast, and buy twice as many beverages as we think we need.

# wine

Here's our big tip: go with the bottle with the cork.

But other than that, we hesitate to tell you too much about the wines you select. Wine is very personal and taste-dependent. One important piece of advice: don't be intimidated by wine.

Unless you have invited a sommelier to dinner, most people don't know that much about wine (even if they think they do).

If you have invited a sommelier, ask him or her to suggest the wines! Otherwise:

- Experiment—try new vineyards from new countries.
- Find a good local liquor store with a knowledgeable staff and ASK, ASK, ASK.
- Read books or magazines on wine.

The "rules" aren't set in stone, but if you want direction, bear in mind the following. Red wines, like Cabernet, Merlot, Pinot Noir, Chianti, Bordeaux and Beaujolais generally go best with heavier meals, red meats and cool weather. (However, Beaujolais goes well with turkey on Thanksgiving, so there goes that rule.) White wines, like Pinot Grigio, Chardonnay and Sauvignon Blanc are associated with warmer temperatures, lighter meals, lighter meats and daylight. Have a bottle or two of Rosé, like Zinfandel, on hand for guests who prefer them. Someone usually does.

As far as glasses go, forget expensive. If you are afraid they'll break, you'll never use them, and then what would the point be? Loosen up! Buy glasses that you are comfortable with, use the right glasses for the beverage when you can, but don't have a coronary if you can't.

Note: Serving nonalcoholic beverages like soda or water in stemware often makes guests who aren't drinking alcohol feel more festive.

# bubbly

Champagne is often relegated to celebrations. "We got funding, crack open the Champagne!" We think drinking Champagne can make a celebration—no excuses necessary. When serving Champagne as an aperitif, calculate two flutes per person (there are six flutes per bottle).

**A Direct Hit**

On New Year's Eve several years ago, we actually witnessed a guest receive a real black eye from a flying Champagne bottle cork. Playing it up, Mr. Thumbs* was smoothly unwrapping a bottle of Champagne when suddenly, there was a pop. The cork rifled through the air at a death-defying speed, over the centerpiece, over the table, and smack into the left eye of our friend, Monique.*

*\* Names have been changed to protect the innocent.*

## a lesson for our friend "mr. thumbs"— six steps for opening a bottle of Champagne without maiming your friends

**1** Take off the foil wrapping (no danger yet).
**2** Grab a kitchen towel and wrap it loosely around the top of the bottle.
**3** Reaching under the towel, grasp the small loop on the wire cage and twist to loosen the cage.

**4** Gently remove the cage.

**5** Hold on to the cork with the towel and turn the bottle until you feel the cork start to give.

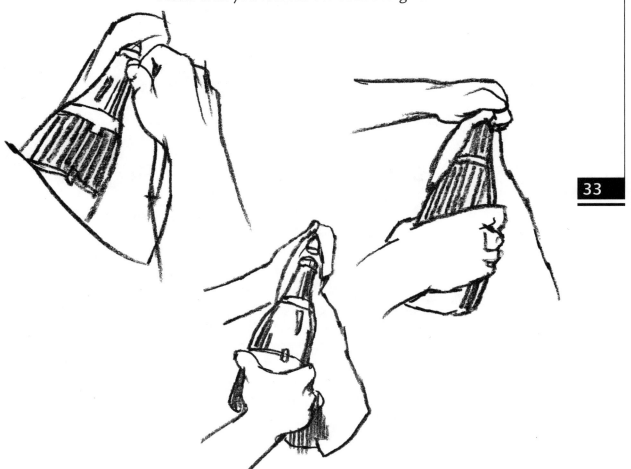

33

**6** Releasing pressure a bit, let the cork push itself out of the bottle and into the towel.

Once you've figured out how to open a bottle of Champagne safely, you can ditch the towel and move on to more advanced techniques. Just remember to always point the bottle AWAY from people, pets and glassware!

# good endings

Don't you hate it when a good movie ends badly? No matter how good the rest of the film, you leave the theater feeling like you've wasted two hours.

If you don't want your guests to leave with that same feeling, consider serving after-dinner drinks. Whether Port, Poire William or Scotch, after-dinner drinks make for a much more satisfying ending to any evening. Offer your guests a selection (it doesn't need to be a big selection—just offering Port is nice), pour the drinks and move away from the dining room table. It's a great way to continue the conversation and give an evening a fresh start.

# space

If you combine your own personal style with things that make your guests feel special and comfortable, you will achieve a graceful, elegant balance in your space. The space in which you entertain should be:

- Comfortable
- Inviting
- Personal

When you prepare a space for a party, try to think of what you are doing as thoughtful, not decorative. Remember, you shouldn't be trying to impress anyone; doing so usually only results in clutter.

Try to keep in mind what you are trying to achieve and adjust the space accordingly.

Do you want people to stay a long time, relaxing and talking? Provide plenty of comfortable seating, a place to put feet up, and dim the lights.

Want people to mingle? Be sure the flow of the space accommodates plenty of movement, and keep the lights brighter. You get the picture.

# hello

Be sure that the entrance to your party is welcoming, clean and not treacherous. Parking should be as accessible and orderly as possible. The walkway leading to your space should be safe, appealing and clean. The entrance to the space should be inviting. This is the first impression your guests get of your party.

# flow

Walk through your party space. Get a feel for it. Don't be afraid to move furniture, tables, even pictures. Make sure that your guests can move freely and easily, and that the flow directs them where you want them to go.

One trick is to have a party, then see where your guests moved your furniture. Did they slide chairs to be closer to the sofa? Did they move a coffee table slightly? If so, do what they did before your next party begins.

## reality check

### candles: cool or creepy?

A few lit candles can make everything look better, but too many candles can look like a séance. Not to mention, if a bunch of different scented candles are used, they can stink.

### tips for using candles:

- Use them sparingly.
- Only use them at night.
- Don't put them on the ground or under things.
- Don't put them on the back of a toilet.
- Avoid using candles if kids will be present.
- Use unscented candles in dining areas.

# focus

Try to bring out the best in the space with which you are working. What part of the space is most appealing? A piece of artwork? A room? A garden? A view? Focus your party on the aspect you most enjoy and which works best for your party. This means arranging furniture or seating in a certain manner, altering the flow of the space to lead your guests toward your focused area, and so on.

## ten tips on party space

**1** Hot rooms make people sleepy, while cool air can keep them awake.

**2** Unless your view is hideous, open your curtains and blinds, even at night.

**3** Remove decorative pillows from couches if you expect people to sit down.

**4** If you don't put out coasters, expect rings on your tabletops.

**5** Know this: your floors are going to get dirty.

**6** Whatever you do, do not burn incense when people are in your home.

**7** Don't light a fire in a fireplace unless it's cold outside.

**8** Check for all kinds of smells, including food and pets, and air out accordingly.

**9** Be sure the space is as neat as you want it to be.

**10** If you prize any particular items in your home, put them away (or don't allow yourself to fixate on them).

# outside

If the event will be held outdoors entirely, there is a whole set of circumstances to consider. Depending on the weather, season and time of day, you may need:

- A tent
- Seating and tables
- Fans
- Sunblock
- Bug spray
- Extra sunglasses
- Blankets
- Coats
- A heater
- Umbrellas
- Benadryl
- Lighting

Outdoor parties require special care for food too, so remember to plan on heat and bugs and bring containers for food storage and cooling.

If there's a beautiful view, a gorgeous tree or a breathtaking body of water, take advantage of it. Let outdoor parties feel like outdoor parties.

Trying to make an outdoor space feel like an elegant indoor one is challenging, and can be quite costly. You're competing with Mother Nature, after all, so take advantage of the natural beauty of the site and ensure that your guests can be comfortable. This means telling your guests ahead of time that the party will be held outdoors, so they can dress accordingly (no high heels, for example).

# table

Aside from food, here's where people get really nervous. Don't. Having a wonderful table does not require living moss or grass, elaborate miniature gifts at each place, or strobe lights under the table. Be yourself. Put out what you have. Just be sure your guests have what they need.

*Have no fear of perfection. You'll never reach it.*

Salvador Dalí

Your guests don't sit down at your table (or approach your buffet) to admire it. They have come to eat.

## ten table tips

1 If you don't have enough place settings, mix. Just be sure your guests have what they need.

2 Cloth napkins are preferable. They don't need to match or be pressed, just neatly folded. A simple rectangle is wonderful.

3 While paper napkins work, try to avoid using them with sticky or messy food, since they tend to disintegrate.

4 If you use plastic utensils, don't serve something difficult to cut.

5 Be sure your chairs are steady.

6 Be sure your guests have enough room to breathe (and, preferably, move).

7 Always put out salt and pepper.

8 Avoid containers (like catsup or butter tubs). Serve such items in bowls or on plates.

9 Always have a pitcher of ice water on the table or nearby.

10 Low candles plus family style serving equals burnt sleeves.

# reality check

## centerpieces for real life

Centerpieces can seem overwhelming. Don't let them be.

The easiest and one of the most attractive centerpieces available is one type of flower, in one color, cut the same length and in a simple vase. It's stunning, inexpensive, and takes about seven minutes.

### basics on centerpieces:

- The centerpiece is not a conversation piece.
- It does not need to be a work of art—you're probably going to remove it when people sit to eat, anyway.
- If you want to keep it on the table, keep it low so guests can see each other.
- If it's tall or bushy, take it off the table before food is served.
- Potted plants work nicely. Anything from flowering plants to cacti look great, and last a lot longer than cut flowers.
- And remember: simple is best.
- But none is fine.

# setting

Table setting is one area where etiquette is key. People are more comfortable when they know where things will be. By standardizing where items are placed, nobody reaches for a fork and finds, say, a sharp knife.

Use the following etiquette rules when setting your table. Exceptions are fine, just don't stray so far that your guests have to ask where the napkin is. To adjust for your meals, simply eliminate unnecessary utensils (for example, if you're not serving soup, don't set out a soupspoon). In fact, be sure you don't set out utensils you won't need just because they look good—you'll confuse people. As you can see, this is just logical. There is an order of use, even for glasses.

# where it all goes

- The dinner plate is centered in front of the guest.
- Flatware is set on either side of the plate in order of use, from the outside in:

    Forks on the left, knives and soupspoon on the right.
- The knife blade faces in, so the guest doesn't inadvertently cut himself.
- The dessert spoon and fork are above the plate, centered, with the spoon over the fork, the spoon facing the diner's left, the fork to the right.
- The bread and butter plate rests above the forks, with the butter knife on the plate, its blade facing inward.
- The napkin is to the left of the forks or on top of the plate. Just don't put it under utensils.

- Glasses rest to the upper right of the plate, over the knife and soupspoon:

    > The water goblet is largest and set most toward the center of the plate (still slightly to the right).

    > To the right of the water glass is the red wineglass, then slightly to the right of that, the white wineglass sits.

    > The Champagne flute sits slightly behind these and to the right a little.

- Salt and pepper are placed on the table, one pair for every two to four people.

# place cards

Place cards aren't necessary but can be helpful. The most important thing to remember about seating arrangements is this: they are not a game—be nice and considerate.

- Without place cards, it is fine to seat people in alternating sex order (boy-girl-boy-girl). This gets people seated quickly, and most people don't mind it (especially if they can choose which "boy" or "girl" sits next to them).
- If you choose not to use place cards, don't let your guests mill around the table, lost—give them direction.

- We think separating spouses at different tables is inconsiderate. Some entertaining experts disagree. (They claim that spousal separation inspires conversation. We're still freshly married.) Be your own judge.

- Never seat people maliciously (like seating a divorced couple near each other) to "stir the pot." Few people enjoy witnessing an argument.

- Seat people with similar interests near one another.

- Be kind and respect your guests.

**48**

# reality check

### wedding singers

We often hear of brides (and other hosts) seating good conversationalists at the most "challenging" tables—you know the table—where the groom's boss, the deaf great-aunt and the aspiring rock star with the big-haired girlfriend sit together, lost in awkward silence.

The more social guests often get seated at such tables in order to "jump start"

conversation. Sounds reasonable, right? Wrong.

Your guests should not work. Few people actually want the job of resuscitating dead tables; they want to have fun.

Don't use your seating arrangements as tools. Remember why your guests are there; make them happy, don't give them jobs.

# precious

Your "good" crystal and china, along with all of your other "good" things, are meant to be used, so use them. What are you saving them for, the next Christie's auction? The value of an item is in the enjoyment it gives people. Share your most prized items with your guests. Hang your art on your wall.

If you choose to share, however, don't spend the evening worrying. And if someone breaks or spills on a special item, remember: nothing is as valuable as the people in your life, and almost everything is replaceable.

But if you feel that something isn't replaceable (i.e., if it has major sentimental value or is far too costly for you to ever replace), by all means put it away in a safe place before the party.

# the host

One last—and vital—part of preparation is preparing the host. A good part of communication is physical; your reactions, eyes and presence have a huge affect on your guests.  No matter how you try to hide inner turmoil or stress, your guests will likely sense them.

We once planned a party as an incentive to finishing a home improvement project. While we had prepared for the party, we were painting baseboards when the first guests arrived. Close friends of ours, they didn't mind in the least and were happy to watch us finish up (after we'd gotten them their drinks, of course). We, on the other hand, were exhausted. Don't forget to leave time to prepare yourself.

Often, that means leaving some last-minute party preparations until you've gotten yourself relaxed and ready. Stop chopping or setting the table and do what you need to do to relax.

- Have a cup of coffee, or a drink.
- Take a nap.
- Exercise.
- Take a shower or bath.
- Get dressed and ready.
- Then finish up.

# do this
## and thank us in the morning

When you get time during your day of preparations, take a minute to do the following.

These four things to do before the party will make your life after the party infinitely nicer:

1 Empty all trashcans and put fresh bags in them.
2 Run then empty the dishwasher.
3 Clear off your kitchen counters as best as possible.
4 Clear a section on your kitchen counter for dirty dish stacking.

# kiss

Last but not least, if you are co-hosting with another person, especially your significant other, try extremely hard not to fight with them before the party. Tension and stress levels are high right before an event. If you do happen to fight, take the time to straighten things out before your guests arrive. Do not wait until after the party to fix the problem. No matter how expert an actor you may be, your guests will sense the tension. Resolve your differences early.

Remember, for your guests to be happy, first you need to be happy.

# grace

*Gracefulness has been defined to be the outward expression of the inward harmony of the soul.*

William Hazlett

# grace

An orchid. A swan. A feather, floating.

Many things come to mind when the word grace is mentioned, although party throwing is usually not one of them. But please roll with us.

Entertaining inevitably involves fiascoes—it is impossible to entertain without something going awry. Things burn. People spill beverages. Adults get drunk, children scrape their knees, dogs eat hors d'oeuvres . . . you name it, and it can go wrong at a party (especially if you think it's important). Because we're all human, there will always be error. Because of this, a graceful host is the most important element in a party.

No matter how good the cheese or how high the soufflé, if the host doesn't possess grace, the party won't reach its potential. By grace, we aren't referring to perfect posture or the ability to prance down a catwalk. In *Webster's Universal College Dictionary*, grace is defined as:

- Elegance or beauty of form, manner, motion, or action;
- Favor, or goodwill;
- Decency or propriety;
- Attractive ease.

As you can see, all of these definitions apply to the aspirations of every host. Gracious hospitality is a much more memorable gift than any labor-intensive trinket. Graceful hosts make everyone feel welcome, important, and at ease. If this sounds familiar, it's because it is. Gracious hosting is guest-centric hosting. This all hinges on two things.

One: stay true to yourself. Be comfortable. Be happy. Above all, be yourself. Joy is contagious. Originality and self-confidence are inspiring.

*That so few dare to be eccentric marks the chief danger of the time.*

John Stuart Mill

Two: etiquette. Really, don't flip the page. We're not contradicting ourselves here by telling you to be yourself and conform to etiquette. That's because etiquette is commonsensical, and acting appropriately never goes out of style. And it doesn't mean you can't be your own wacky self.

Etiquette and grace go hand-in-hand. But please remember that nobody can be the living, breathing embodiment of grace. Nobody is perfect and everyone has flaws. Some of us are very self-possessed but might not be so thoughtful. Some of us are thoughtful but lack self-confidence. And some of us are completely self-absorbed with no confidence whatsoever. (We're kidding.) The point is: we're all human. So be graceful to yourself as well.

Being a graceful host is important in every moment of party planning:

- Before
- During
- After

# before

## guests

Remember to choose your guest list wisely. Don't invite people who don't get along—or, for larger gatherings where this is inevitable, don't seat them together. Try to invite or seat people together who would enjoy one another's company: people with similar interests, likes and dislikes. Invite people who would like (or have asked) to meet one another. Try to include guests' dates, so people don't have to come alone.

## planning

Remember to be graceful about where and when the party will take place. Consider your guests' needs. Make sure the space will be accessible to everyone—physically and logistically. Be sure everyone will be comfortable.

Be considerate of the time. If you know most of your guests need to retire early, plan to accommodate that need. If you know they'll want to be staying out until all hours, don't start the party until later in the evening. If it's very hot outside,

consider having your party later in the day, when it's cooler. Or plan on having plenty of shade and lots of drinks.

Be flexible. If you know there's an event that follows your own, don't get upset, go with it. This happens often during the holidays, and people tend to get bent out of shape. Why bother? Why would you alienate or even lose guests over another event? What do you care? Start your party earlier and have it in a place that helps those who need to get to the other party.

Similarly, don't schedule your party for a time you know conflicts with someone else's party. If someone you know always has a Halloween party, and most of your friends usually attend that party, don't usurp the date by deciding to throw your own Halloween party. You'll only make your friends uncomfortable. Remember, entertaining isn't a popularity contest.

# invitations

Always include everyone you intend to invite in your invitations. Don't send out formal invitations and then, to save a few bucks, call your closest friends. Send them the invitation too. They're special. Don't treat your closer friends like they don't matter when inviting people. Double—and for large gatherings triple—check your invitation lists to be sure you're not forgetting anyone.

> When we got married, we forgot to send an invitation to Ron's best man.

Include everyone you want at your party on the envelope. If you want kids, invite them. If you want dates to come, be sure they're on the envelope. Don't assume people will know whom you wish to have at your party.

If you don't specify—and someone brings kids to your formal dinner party—don't even think about getting upset. (FYI: the kids won't ruin the night—but if you get upset or react negatively to their presence, you certainly will.)

# rsvps

Be sure you've given a reasonable response date and give a few days' leeway on responses. Don't select a response date that's too close to the event so that you're frantic if a few people haven't called the day after your response deadline. Give yourself—and your guests—a bit of breathing room.

> We once received an invitation to a party that was held at a restaurant. The hostess called us a week before the RSVP date to find out if we were attending. At first we thought we had made an error and missed a response date, but when we double-checked the invitation, we discovered we hadn't. If you give a response date, please don't expect people to respond early. If you find out you need a response earlier than you'd expected, admit the mistake when you call for a response so your guests don't feel like they goofed.

## seven rsvp tips

**1** Don't call your invitees the day after the response date asking for a response. When you do call (a few days later), be gracious. They probably just forgot.

**2** Don't berate people for not responding, and don't make them feel guilty in a sneaky way. Be straightforward and be understanding.

**3** When invitees decline, let them off the hook. Don't ask them why they can't come, and don't go overboard fussing about how you'll miss them. Just because you invited someone doesn't make you privy to the reason they can't attend. Simply tell them you are sorry they can't come and that you hope to see them soon.

**4** Similarly, when someone declines and stammers their way through a ridiculous excuse, let them do it and be gracious about it.

**5** Don't try to catch anyone in a lie and point it out. That's simply rude.

**6** Never, ever mention an invitee's excuse for not attending to the other guests in attendance at your party.

**7** In short, be kind. You don't win anything by being mean.

# additions **and** subtractions

If an invitee asks if they can bring an uninvited guest, be considerate and thoughtful. We automatically say "yes." We feel that if a guest takes the time and musters up the nerve to ask, it must be important to them. If your situation doesn't permit additions, when the guest asks, just provide a straightforward, honest response. Try not to make the guest feel guilty for asking.

The same stands for subtractions—last-minute withdrawals. If someone has something come up at the last minute, accept their decline and go on with the party. Do not make them feel badly. They probably had a hard time declining—they've likely suffered enough. And if they decline at the last moment regularly, address the issue with them after the event.

It isn't your job to administer etiquette lessons to your guests. Be understanding, try your best to accommodate them, and forge ahead with your plans.

# assistance

Often, invitees offer assistance. They offer to make dishes, help by bringing something or coming over early, and so forth. You may or may not want this help. The most important thing you can do is be honest. If you want help, accept it. If you don't want help, decline. Just remember to do so nicely and tactfully.

For those invitees who won't take a polite "no" for an answer, just accept what they're offering and move on. If they're dead-set on bringing their specialty Jell-o mold, so be it. Let them bring it and let them be proud. In the long run, who cares if it looks funny on your buffet? Make it look as nice as possible and then accept it as part of your guest's personality. Your guest is more important.

**66**

# phone calls

One of the more trying parts of entertaining are the phone calls hosts receive the day of the party. People call to ask "how you're doing," or "how the cooking's coming along," or to offer last-minute help. While it's very hard to remember this as you're juggling the phone while chopping tomatoes and running a Cuisinart: they mean well. Be as polite as you can and get off the phone as quickly as possible. Most people understand when you tell them you're busy preparing but are excited to see them and catch up with them at the party.

## early birds

Like death and taxes, early birds are pretty much inevitable. No matter how prepared you are someone is more prepared than you. Sadly, at these times you must resist the urge to pretend you aren't home.

If you're not ready, remain calm and composed. Of course you expected to greet the first guests in your robe with no makeup on. Here's what you do.

- Greet them warmly.
- Offer and get them drinks and put out a few hors d'oeuvres.
- Tell them to make themselves at home.
- Get yourself ready.

# during

The most important—and often most challenging—time to be graceful is while your party is occurring.

Like we said earlier, disasters are bound to happen. Throwing a party can often feel like juggling—like juggling eggs, a brick and a working chainsaw, no less—but do your best to remember that everything will work out. The most important thing to always keep in mind is the enjoyment of your guests (one more time, guest-centric). Then act gracefully no matter what occurs.

Really: if the main course burns to a crisp, would anyone mind ordering in pizza and a salad? We say not!

But gracious hosting involves more than just recovering from a burned filet mignon. Things break, guests act rudely, people bring uninvited guests and—yes, it's happened to us more than once—dogs suddenly appear. These are the times when being graceful seems impossible, and yet it's most important.

# greetings

For small gatherings, greet every guest that arrives at your door. Welcome them into your home, and immediately take their coats, hats and so forth, so they're not standing awkwardly in your doorway wearing overcoats while everyone else is in cocktail attire.

Once they're inside and comfortable, invite them into the group. This means, introduce them to guests they might enjoy, reintroduce them to guests they may have already met, or, if the gathering is extremely small, introduce them to the whole bunch. It's better to reintroduce someone if you're not sure they know one another, rather than expect them to know the other guests.

Once they're in and introduced, immediately offer them a drink—and get it for them right away. Don't let them say like our late Uncle Jerry often jokingly did, "I've been here twenty minutes and no one's offered me a drink!" (Of course, Uncle Jerry usually said that the minute he walked in the door, but you get the point.)

For larger parties, you may not be available by the door, so you have to approach greetings differently.

- If you have help during the party, have them greet people at the door, take coats and either offer drinks or point out the bar.
- If you don't have that kind of (or any) help, do your best to swoop by the door as often as possible to check on guests as they arrive.
- If you find even swooping by the door is challenging (this happens at very large parties), make sure to seek everyone out and take the time to talk to everyone briefly, early on in the evening.
- Remember: work the party. You wanted them to come, so you should talk to them.

# introductions

Introductions should be handled with care. Bungling introductions happens, and when it does, just apologize.

But when you introduce people, try to keep these generalities in mind.

- Always try to say, "Robert Winter, I'd like you to meet Connie Smith," or, "Robert Winter, this is Connie Smith." Rather than the repetitive and kind of annoying: "Robert Winter, Connie Smith. Connie Smith, Robert Winter."

- It is nice to say something personal about the person you are introducing, such as "Bob, I'd like you to meet my childhood friend, John." It shows familiarity.
- It is also considerate to introduce younger people to older people such as, "Mr. Wilson, I'd like to introduce Chuckie Johnson to you."
- It is a lot nicer to use full names.
- If you flub an introduction and are corrected by the guest, apologize and move on. The guest, hopefully, will have enough tact not to correct you in a condescending way. If they are critical, try to forgive them; they're probably just insecure.

# late arrivals

Late guests don't need to disrupt the whole party—and they won't if you don't let them (or make them). Waiting everything for them only calls attention to their tardiness and will make them feel more uncomfortable. Fifteen minutes is the maximum you need to hold dinner for a guest; most of us have cocktail time before dinner, so if the guest isn't there by the established time for dinner—usually an hour or more after the start of the party—plus fifteen minutes, they're pretty late.

- When the late guest does arrive, greet them charmingly and don't get upset that they're late.
- Assume they had a good reason (and don't ask).

# reality check

## shoeless joes

Recently, we were invited to a party in the middle of winter with snow on the ground, where the hosts opened their garage door and posted a sign asking all guests to remove their snow-laden shoes before entering the house.

We were not pre-warned, so guests spent most of the evening apologizing for mismatched socks and old pedicures. To leave, we had to walk on a wet, freezing concrete garage floor in our socks or stocking feet and search through a mountain of freezing wet shoes to find our shoes.

Even if you have babies crawling on your floor, please don't subject your guests to this. Don't have a party if you're so worried about your kids or your carpet.

If it's a cultural tradition, that's fine. But at least consider providing clean slippers, or, if your party's in the winter or on a rainy day, giving your guests little towels so their feet don't freeze or get wet on the way out. And put your "shoeless policy" on the invitation, so guests can at least wear nice socks or get their toenails painted.

- Make the late guest comfortable, introduce them and get them a drink, and serve them whatever course they've arrived during, unless it's dessert, in which case it's nicer to offer them the main course while everyone else is eating dessert. You can always ask them what they'd prefer. If they'd rather skip the main course, that's okay, too.

- Your goal here should simply be to make the late arrival and the other guests as comfortable as possible.

# **unexpected** guests

Sometimes, uninvited guests appear, and essentially, it's the host's job to welcome them into the party. Invitees bring unannounced guests, neighbors stop by, friends who "heard about the party" drop in, and so forth. It may be awkward, but it happens, and as a host, you're going to have to deal with it. The solution is simple.

Invite them in and be happy that they are there.

Don't be uncomfortable or angry (or if you are, don't let on). If you get upset, it makes the people you invited very uneasy. In fact, if you can decide prior to every party that if anyone unexpected shows up it would make you extremely happy—then you won't get upset, you'll welcome them with open arms. And that's how it should be. An unexpected guest is still a guest.

- Welcome them, greet them, involve them in the party.
- Get them a drink, a chair, a party hat.
- Set them a place at the table.

- If a buffet, be sure there are enough plates, utensils and napkins to accommodate them.
- Thank them for coming to your party.

# gifts

When someone brings you a hostess gift, be thankful. If it is a wrapped present, try opening it in their presence—without making too big a fuss. (If you do, those who didn't bring gifts will feel badly.) If it's something you could use during the party, by all means do so. It'll please the giver. If it's decorative—like a candleholder—display it nicely. Even if it's not to your liking, put it out. You can always put it away the next day.

If it's a food item, like a dessert, ask them if they would like you to serve it to your guests. Unless it would taste awful with the other food you're serving, of course, in which case you should thank the giver profusely and let them know you'll eat it tomorrow.

If the gift is a bottle of wine or liquor, offer to serve it. If you have already planned the beverage menu carefully, explain this to the giver and thank them, assuring them you are excited to try their selection.

If a guest brings flowers, no matter how they "go" with your décor or other flower arrangements, thank the guest and put

74

the flowers lovingly in an appropriate vase with water, and display them in a flattering place. Please don't let fresh flowers wilt by not taking care of them. This would not only insult the giver, but Mother Nature as well.

# going **fishing**

Very few things are more awkward than a host fishing for a compliment. Guests never know what to say (what if they don't like what you're showing them?) and most would rather be enjoying the party. After all, they didn't come over for a house or new furniture tour. They came for a party.

*Friendship without self-interest is one of the rare beautiful things in life.*

James F. Byrnes

Don't use your guests to bolster your self-image. Don't give unsolicited house tours, unless your home is so gigantic you think guests might get lost. Ditto for garden tours, and please avoid dragging people in to see the "fabulous new marble right off the dock from Italy" in your bathroom. No matter how proud you are, try to resist pointing out or showing off new acquisitions.

That said, if a guest asks for a tour, or to see your new bathroom sink, then by all means—show her! When we're at other people's homes, we often ask to see things, especially when we know they've been working on something or just bought something new. It can be a nice way to start off an evening.

Just try not to drag people around unless they ask.

# smoking

If there's a hot topic in entertaining, it's smoking. This is simplified when entertaining outside the home because the rule is dictated by the establishment, city or state. Whether or not one should allow guests to smoke freely in one's home seems much trickier—and yet it has a very obvious, simple answer.

If you are hosting at home, do what pleases you, just be sure that all of your guests can be comfortable. This isn't very complicated—and it goes for cigars and pipes, as well as cigarettes.

We always allow smoking in our home because we find it makes many of our guests more comfortable. We want all of our guests to feel free to be themselves, and to enjoy themselves. Plus, we find it highly distracting to force people to leave the party to feel comfortable! We have found that most nonsmokers don't mind the smoke, especially if it's handled considerately (by opening windows or turning on an air purifier).

The way we see it, you have two options.

1 If you don't mind people smoking in your home, then put ashtrays out around the house and let those who've got 'em, smoke 'em. Do set aside a comfortable nonsmoking area—and direct those who dislike smoke to that spot. Air the place out occasionally, and clean out ashtrays regularly.

2 On the flip side, if you absolutely cannot stand smoke or if you or someone in your home is asthmatic, establish a smoking area somewhere comfortable outside (preferably in an enclosed area, like a porch, with seating). Be sure to provide ashtrays or other appropriate receptacles.

Whatever you do, don't criticize a guest for wanting to smoke, just because you don't partake. Smoking isn't illegal.

Accommodate smokers to your best ability. Don't prohibit people from smoking in or around your home. If you do, they'll spend your whole party wishing they were somewhere else.

Contrarily, if you smoke, don't fill up every available party space with smoke and full ashtrays, so that your nonsmoking guests spend the evening trying to find fresh air.

It isn't your job to teach your guests a lesson. In either case (smoking or non)—don't make your guests suffer—make them happy.

# children

If you have invited children to your party, you should have things on hand to entertain them, and if you haven't invited any, have a few child-friendly items on hand in case someone brings their child in error. Crayons and paper are an easy solution.

If the kids are happy, the parents are usually happy.

For parties that include children, you might want to have one or more of the following (depending on the size and location of the party . . . for example, at an indoor child-friendly party there should not be a football—you'd be asking for trouble!):

Board games
Piñata
Toys
Hula Hoops
Sporting equipment
Napping space and pillows

We have had several piñatas at our parties, particularly our annual Fourth of July parties. Surprisingly, our most manly single bachelors are the ones who get the most involved in the piñata set-up and operation! It's always a terrific time, watching our friends set up and man the piñata, while the kids line up and take turns swatting at it, then scamper around finding candy.

We have noticed, however, that we tend to start the piñata festivities a little too late (without children of our own, we forget how early very little kids go to bed). Be sure to attend to piñatas or other children-focused events early enough for even the youngest to enjoy them.

For adult-focused parties with several children, consider hiring a babysitter (or more than one). If you don't know any, call people you know with kids and ask for recommendations. Tips for accommodating babysitters at parties:

- Set an area where the children will be with the sitter(s).
- Instruct the sitters not to interrupt the party unless truly necessary.

- Have plenty of toys, games and activities to keep the kids occupied.
- Have one babysitter per every four children. Babysitters are quickly outnumbered, especially when parents are nearby and kids are determined.

## infants

If guests bring infants, be sure to provide a place for the parents to store their baby supplies, as well as a place for changing and/or feeding the babies and space for the babies to lie down.

## pets

Some people bring pets to parties. We never object (we love animals), but not everyone feels the same way we do. So what to do when someone brings Sparky to your next event?

Let the pooch in, and treat old Sparky like he's the guest's child. Yes, do this even if the dog has muddy paws, bad breath and fleas—and you dislike dogs. That dog is now your guest. Set out a bowl of water and start petting your new buddy. That said—if you have pets and are having a party—put them away. Now.

A few words about your pet . . .

Nobody likes your pet as much as you do.

People are allergic, afraid, or simply don't appreciate your pet. In special circumstances it is okay to introduce your pet to a small crowd. Briefly. Otherwise, give your pet a treat, put them in a comfortable, safe place, and be very attentive to them after the party.

# accidents

If you entertain, accidents will happen. Nobody's perfect. There are two types of accidents that happen at parties: those caused by your guests, and those you cause yourself. Both should be handled as nonchalantly and as caringly as possible.

When a guest breaks something, spills something or otherwise makes a mess, handle it in this order:

1 Be sure they're okay.
2 If they are, and they apologize, accept their apology and ensure that your guest knows that the accident is not a problem (rarely is any accident really a big deal).
3 Clean up the mess as quickly and as unobtrusively as possible.
4 Replace the broken item (i.e., if it's the guest's wineglass, get them a new one, and so forth).
5 Get on with the party as soon as you can.

If you break something, spill something or otherwise make a mess where guests are present, find out if anyone is hurt and if not, apologize for the mess and quickly clean it up. If you burn something or otherwise ruin a dish, first decide whether or not that dish is important (if not, toss it and forget about it) and if it is—replace it.

84

On the night of a big storm we decided to throw a large impromptu fondue party, because we were one of the few homes in our area with electrical power. That is, ours was the house with power—until our guests arrived, the power went out and the house went dark.

We lit all the candles we had and started a fire, but there was nothing we could do about the food—we have an electric stovetop. For a moment we thought we were out of luck, but our neighbors (who also happened to be at the party) have a gas stove. So we walked the food next door, cooked it, walked it back, and ate fondue by candlelight.

On top of the trekking back and forth with the food, our basement "wine cellar" flooded without our knowledge, and when we went to grab a few bottles for dinner, we found them floating. With no labels. Instead of panicking, we proceeded to have a "wine tasting" party. We had no idea which were our better bottles of wine and which were our cheapest. Everyone had a ball—and got absolutely looped—trying to guess which wines were the best.

An evening of total disaster resulted in a great story—
for everyone there—for years to come.

# rude behavior

It's difficult when a guest acts rudely. A little tolerance goes
a long way, but too much tolerance puts the rude person
in control, and the rest of the guests (host included) at a
disadvantage. Bad etiquette is one thing (eating sloppily and so
forth), but aggressive or knowingly rude behavior (ranging from
name calling to unacceptable touching to bigotry or threatening
behavior) is totally unacceptable and should not be tolerated.

You invited them; it's your job to put a stop to them. At some
point, you might have to ask a rude guest to stop behaving
badly and let them know that if they don't, they're going to
have to leave. If they've insulted someone, try to smooth things
over. Always keep in mind that it's better to have one upset
guest than twenty uncomfortable or unhappy ones.

If you have to ask your guest to leave, do it alone with them,
out of earshot. Don't make a scene and don't embarrass the
rude guest or put him or her on the spot. It's not very nice,
and rude behavior doesn't justify rudeness back. If the
behavior doesn't stop, quietly and discreetly ask the person to
leave. If they are drunk and have a sober companion, speak
with the sober companion. If they have been drinking and are
alone, call a taxi.

# illness and injury

Guests sometimes get sick or hurt. Whatever you do, don't get "put out" when this happens. You might be directly in the middle of pulling that fabulous soufflé out of the oven when your guest complains of a terrible headache, or when they cut their finger.

Drop what you are doing—no matter what it is—and care for your hurt or sick guest.

It is a good idea to have basic medical products on hand and easy to find. The following three things solve a number of problems:

1 Aspirin and other over-the-counter painkillers
2 Benadryl (works wonders for food allergies)
3 Tums

If someone gets sick and needs to lie down, offer a bed. Clear it off if you must, but take care of your guest.

# serving the meal

It can be a hectic time, right when the meal is ready to be served. Try your best to relax and get organized, and take a deep breath. For sit-down dinners, when the meal is about ready, light your candles and fill your water glasses. If you have a buffet, get all of the cold dishes onto the buffet table. Then, as the hot dishes are finished, transfer them onto pre-warmed dishes or onto heating trays on the buffet.

When you are ready, ask your guests to be seated. If you have too many guests to do this yourself, ask for help. Once everyone is seated, if you are serving the meal yourself, remember to serve from the left, remove from the right. If you can't follow this rule, don't sweat it. Serve yourself last.

## fifteen serving tips

1 If serving family-style (large platters being passed), be sure every guest can hold each of the platters. If a platter is too heavy or too hot, carry it around the table yourself, holding it for your guests.

2 Don't forget that every platter needs appropriate and easy-to-use serving utensils. For example, try not to put a short spoon in soft food, where the handle might sink and get messy.

3 Dishes should be passed in one direction to avoid confusion.

4 Guests can pass condiments and bread on their own, even with plated meals.

5 Remember that hosts must lead. Announce that it is okay to begin eating if food is getting cold, or lift your fork and start, to indicate that it is appropriate for others to do so. Guests look to you for instruction, don't forget this.

**6** If a buffet, offer to plate the food for elderly people or those who physically can't do it themselves.

**7** Remember to keep an eye on beverages, and refill glasses when they get empty. You can put beverages on the table for self-service if you like, but keep an eye on your guests and take care of them.

**8** When clearing, don't stack dishes. Carry two at a time. Stacked dishes with food on them are very unsightly and awkward.

**9** Don't scrape plates at or near the table.

**10** Remove everything from the previous course before starting a new one. This includes clearing out used plates after buffet meals.

**11** Don't accept too much help with clearing, or it can get chaotic and you can end up with only two people sitting at the table, bored.

**12** Offer something sweet to eat after dinner. One of our friends says, "I need something sweet to tell me the meal's over."

**13** After-dinner drinks can be offered with coffee and dessert.

**14** You don't need to clear dessert dishes or coffee cups and after-dinner drink glasses from your table. Your job at this point is to keep the party going.

**15** If you have the room, move the party away from the table after dessert, bringing the after-dinner drinks or coffee with you.

## reality check

### after-dinner coffee

After dinner, if you are serving coffee, make it decaffeinated coffee. Ask if guests would prefer "regular" coffee or tea (have a selection).

Never serve caffeinated coffee and tell people it is decaffeinated. Some people have averse reactions to caffeine and most people don't drink it after a certain time simply because it keeps them awake.

Have milk, cream, sugar and a sugar substitute available.

# mealtime etiquette

Think of this as a "refresher course" on basic dining etiquette. Even though many of the following "rules" may seem obvious and a little humorous, they're extremely important.

### twenty things to do while eating or drinking (so you don't offend anybody)

1 Take the swizzle stick out of your drink (you could lose an eye).

2 For that matter, remove the little umbrella and big pineapple slice (or anything else) from your glass, if only because they're kind of dorky.

**3** When offered an appetizer with a toothpick in it, don't put the toothpick back onto the serving platter when you're done. Nobody else wants to use it!

**4** Ditto for shrimp tails.

**5** Never double-dip. Never.

**6** When at the table, start with the utensil that is farthest from the plate.

**7** Say "please" and "thank you."

**8** Don't slouch.

**9** Don't slurp.

**10** Don't rest your elbows on the table while eating. It is okay to put them on the table to lean forward in conversation (so long as there is no food on your plate).

**11** Don't reach across the table like "Stretch Armstrong." Ask people to "please pass the . . ."

**12** When passing, pass both the salt and the pepper together, even if someone only asks for one.

**13** Don't chew with your mouth open or take big bites.

**14** Don't start spearing food from other people's plates. Don't ask, "are you gonna finish that?"— even if the girl with the plate full of food only weighs 98 pounds—eat what's on your plate only.

**15** Please don't feed anybody but yourself, no matter how frisky you're feeling.

**16** Don't tuck your napkin into your shirt or pants, even if you are wearing a white belt, white sandals and head-to-toe polyester.

17 Put your napkin on your chair or draped next to your plate if you have to leave the table. Don't go to great lengths to refold it.

18 On the flip side, please don't ball your napkin up, drop it in the middle of your plate, belch loudly and announce something about having to use the "john."

19 Don't turn your coffee cup upside-down if you don't want coffee. Just say "no thank you."

20 To indicate that you have finished a main course, place the knife and fork diagonally on your plate from top left to lower right.

**92**

# restaurants or clubs

When you're entertaining outside of your home, keep a few things in mind. Most importantly, even more so than in your home, in a restaurant or club, you need to lead. Your guests may be unfamiliar with the place; they may be intimidated or unsure of themselves. You need to help them feel at ease so they can enjoy themselves.

- If you're entertaining at a place with a dress code, be sure to tell your guests the dress code well ahead of time.

- Greet your guests at the door or, if you have secured a private room, standing near the entrance to that room. And if you are seated when latecomers arrive, stand for them.

- About drinks: if your club works on a tab system, let your guests know this ahead of time so they don't try to pay the bartender and look silly standing there with money.  Similarly, in either a restaurant or club, don't let your guests buy their own drinks. Just let them know they can order freely and that it's all been taken care of. Act generously, and forget about the tab. You decided to come here, didn't you?

- For a large group (eight or more), arrange the menu ahead of time. Most restaurants will print a special menu for you.

- If the service is terrible, never complain loudly to your table. Pulling a "power move" with service people at a dinner only makes you look like a loser, not a "big shot." If something needs straightening out, excuse yourself and address the problem with someone on staff at the facility (away from the table).

- Make payment arrangements ahead of time. Give the staff person with whom you are dealing your credit card and indicate a 20% gratuity before the meal. Let them know you don't want to sign the receipt at the dinner.

- If you haven't arranged to pay in advance, pay for the bill discreetly. Don't accept offers from guests to "help." Not even with the tip.

- See each guest who leaves to the door, and stay until your last guest leaves.

# conversation

Good conversation requires give and take; that means equal parts listening and speaking. (Great conversationalists are great listeners.) Everyone in this world knows more about something than you do, so listen and learn.

Think about what you're about to say before you say it.

Make eye contact. Looking over someone's shoulder while you're talking to them is a tremendous character flaw. You know as well as your guests that there are few things as rude as someone who looks over your shoulder during a conversation.

When seated at a table, don't turn your back on the person sitting next to you to speak to someone on your other side. It's exclusionary and fairly mean to the person who is forced to look at your back, left out of the conversation. Just look at the person you're talking to with your head, turning your shoulders only slightly. Then be sure to engage the person on your other side eventually.

Always try to find common ground, and (unless you know everyone really well), as they say—it's always best to avoid talking about politics and religion.

## ten things to say to people . . .
### if you don't want them to
#### ever speak to you again

1  Have you gained weight?
2  You look tired. (Also: You look bloated.)
3  Why don't you have kids?
4  How much did that cost?
5  Have you found a job yet?
6  You know, you're beginning to look just like your mother.
7  How come you're still single?
8  Did I hear your dog just died?
9  The last time I saw you, you were stumbling drunk.
10  Are you pregnant?

## reality check

### saying grace

If you say grace regularly at your home and are having a small dinner party and would like to say grace, you should. Do try to keep the grace brief and general, and don't be offended if some of your guests decline to join in.

It's a nice idea to preempt your grace by saying that you say it every night and would like to share your tradition with your guests. If anybody objects, give a toast instead.

If a guest asks to say grace but you don't practice that tradition, oblige them. It won't hurt anybody.

## accepting

If a guest arrives at your home in peculiar or what you consider inappropriate attire, don't be bothered. Be tolerant. If a guest has different taste or beliefs than you do, they should be all the more interesting for you to get to know. So if a guest brings a date in head-to-toe leather with face piercings—or, if you and your friends are dressed in leather with body piercings and a guest arrives in head-to-toe Ralph Lauren—embrace the new person as you would any friend, and maybe you'll expand your horizons.

If a guest comes in an inappropriate outfit—they wear a bunny costume to a noncostume cocktail party—you might want to offer them a change of clothes, if they are remotely close in size to you or someone in your home. Be sure not to offer them something out of your "send to Goodwill" bag (i.e., something ratty, mothball smelling or from two decades ago). Offer them something they'll be happy to wear.

We have a friend who lost our invitation to a Halloween party—and she showed up the next weekend—when we weren't having a party—in a gypsy costume. We all got a great laugh out of that one.

# reality check

### telephone use

When someone asks to use your phone, let them, and find them a quiet, out-of-the-way place to talk. Don't let a guest carry on a phone conversation in the middle of a party if you can help it, since it will distract the other guests.

Guests shouldn't feel like they have to use their cell phones in your home (nor should they—it's rude). If they forget themselves and start placing calls, direct them politely to one of your home phones in a private space and tell them to dial direct.

Many guests at summertime parties arrive in shorts and t-shirts. When the sun sets and it cools off, we have extra sweaters and jackets available. Most people won't ask to borrow something, but when offered a warm layer, they will jump at the opportunity. So offer.

## bathrooms

Be sure to provide some kind of hand towels (paper is fine), soap, extra toilet paper and room fragrance. Have a trashcan in the bathroom. Always clean what you don't want your guests to see out of your bathroom. People are curious by nature. Don't punish guests for being human. Just remove any personal effects.

We mentioned this briefly in "foundation": don't put lit candles on the back of your toilets. Guests burn hair and the back of their clothing that way. If you must put a lit candle in the bathroom, find a safe countertop to put it on, where guests (or objects) won't catch fire.

## early departures

Sometimes people have to leave early. Sometimes guests are called with problems at home; sometimes they have other obligations and simply have to leave your party early. Or maybe they're just bored. Who knows? In any case, when they announce to you that they have to leave, be gracious and let them go.

- Don't gush, "Do you really have to go?" It puts the guest in an awkward position (they'd stay if they could or if they wanted to).
- Don't ask them why they're leaving. It isn't your business.
- Retrieve any coats or belongings the guest may have stored in your home, thank them for coming and say goodbye. Then rejoin your guests.

# the end of the **evening**

Some of the best conversations happen after dinner. As we mention earlier in this book, we think you should serve dessert, coffee and after-dinner drinks. They keep the evening going and set you up for a nice finish.

A new setting for after-dinner drinks will rejuvenate or extend great conversation. Changing scenery is always energizing. You might feel more comfortable taking after-dinner drinks outside the dining room. Depending on the time of year, this can mean anywhere: the living room, the family room, out on a dock, on the front porch. If you're spontaneous at the end of the evening, your guests will enjoy your party up until the moment you would like them to leave. Enjoy yourself.

On the flip side, if you're yawning and looking at your watch while they're eating pie, they're going to want to get out of Dodge. And that's the feeling they'll remember. Everything prior to dessert gets overshadowed by how you end the evening.

All you have to do to prevent a bad finish is to remember to enjoy yourself, and add a little kick to the party at the end. It's a lot like those marathon runners you see—they hit some kind of wall, and then they have a sip of water and suddenly they're racing to the finish line. You can do that with your parties, too. Just offer a fresh drink and a change of scenery, and you'll be surprised how you can perk things (and yourself) up.

when you want your guests to leave . . .

- Don't start cleaning up and fussing around. Your guests might get the hint, but they'll think you're kind of rude.
- Do not run the dishwasher. Just don't. Please.
- Don't put pajamas on or do anything similarly frightening.
- Don't let your crazy dogs out into the party and laugh evilly when they eat the leftover dessert off the dining room table.
- Please don't trot out your exhausted, pajama-clad children to sing to the crowd like the kids in *The Sound of Music,* either.
- Don't round up everyone's coats and drop them in the middle of the group and announce, "It's been fun, but you've all got to go."

When you're ready for the party to end, be a leader. Stand up and let everyone know you've had a lovely time, but it's time to retire. It's better to gracefully conclude an evening rather than drop desperate hints.

## guests who won't leave

Inevitably, you will have one (or more) guest who wants to hang around longer than you might wish. The odds of this happening increase dramatically when you choose to make alcohol a focus of your party—particularly mixed drinks. Don't even think about serving margaritas if you don't want people to hang around until dawn.

Of course, not often do you actually want your guests to stay until the wee hours. If you had, you would have called the party a slumber party, right? So what do you do about the guest who won't go home?

If they're at your home really late, it's fairly easy to tell the late-stayer that you're exhausted and it's time for you to go to bed. Usually, you don't have to ask them to leave after saying that, but sometimes you do. Or, if it's a few good friends, you can go to bed and ask them to lock up.

> At our larger parties, there are always a half dozen or so guests milling around at 3:00 A.M. Usually, they start eating about then . . . firing up the grill, digging through the fridge. Often, we're right there with them. But sometimes, we just can't stay awake a moment longer. That's when we tell them we'd love to stay up with them, but we're going to bed. If they want to stay, we ask the sober person in the group (there's usually one) to shut out any lights and lock the door when they leave—and then we go to bed.

If it's not that late in the evening but guests are overstaying their welcome nonetheless, you simply have to let them know the party's over. We prefer a direct method. Say something straightforward such as, "Thank you very much for coming to the party. We've enjoyed ourselves, and look forward to doing this again soon." Unless your guests are thicker than rocks, they'll stand up and get ready to leave.

# after

It would seem as if your requirements are finished once all of your guests leave, wouldn't it? However, there are still a few things that will need your attention.

## remainders

Guests leave things behind. It's kind of like dogs and hair.

From articles of clothing to purses, to children's belongings to dishes, you can expect your guests to leave something behind. You have several options for returning items, depending on the size of your party and how well you know your guests.

For small parties, if you know who left certain items, you can call the guest and let them know they've done so. Schedule a time for them to pick the item up, or leave it in a safe place for them to retrieve later.

Or, dropping off things is nice. If you want to drop the item off at the owner's home, you should call them ahead of time and let them know. Dropping in unexpectedly isn't always a wise idea, even when you're being nice. (This isn't an excuse to drop by for dinner.)

For large parties or when you have no idea whom an item belongs to, you can store the left-behind items in a convenient place and wait for the owners to call to arrange a pickup.

## leftover guests

Occasionally, a guest will have too much to drink or, for some other reason, end up sleeping at your home. Treat them as you would a planned houseguest. When they wake up, provide them with clean towels, a spare (obviously, new) toothbrush and toothpaste, a place to shower and dress, and some aspirin, coffee and water.

It is nice to treat them to breakfast, but not necessary. Offer them coffee, and let them wake up, clean up and get home.

Whatever you do, don't enlist the accidental overnight guest in your cleanup efforts. While it's tempting, having an extra set of hands right at your disposal and all, let the poor person go. Don't put them to work. (Although we once did this with a younger cousin—put him to work cleaning up empties, of all things—but that was to teach him a lesson about drinking.)

## offers

Sometimes, guests offer to help clean up the next day. By and large, we think it's best if you do this yourself. It's your party, and you shouldn't be inconveniencing your guests. But for large parties, when a bunch of close friends offer to help the next day, it can be almost like a second party.

## reality **check**

### garbage

After a party of any size (but especially large ones), check the surroundings of your home for trash or personal belongings. The last thing you want is to leave your party's mark on the neighborhood or the environment.

It is your obligation to clean up after your guests both in your home—and in your neighborhood. Get yourself up out of bed early the morning after a party and pick up any litter left behind.

Clean up after yourself and your guests.

If you have beverages chilled and leftovers ready to eat, your friends can come over, clean up, and relax—all at the same time. Some of our parties reached their high point the next evening.

## borrowed goods

Return any borrowed items sparkling clean—and promptly. Don't take several months to return someone's large coffee maker. Clean everything thoroughly (in the dishwasher, if possible). Have linens or clothing items dry-cleaned. Return items within a week at latest. If someone loaned you something extra special, you might want to consider returning it with a thank-you gift. Even something as easy as some cookies or a bottle of Champagne is perfect.

Remember, you want people to loan you things again.

## thank-you notes

It isn't necessary to send someone a thank-you note for a hostess gift, unless the gift is so thoughtful or special that you feel that you must.

## apologies

If there is anyone who might have been upset during the party—from a guest who had to deal with someone rude, a person you forgot to invite, to your neighbors (if the party got very loud and they didn't come), apologize the very next day. If the offense is severe, bring a gift. Flowers will do. Don't wait to correct any mistakes you or one of your guests made.

# drop-bys

After large parties especially (and in particular if you've done a great job), people might feel inclined just to "drop by" and say hello and thanks. We think this is because when you've had a large party and you've done it right—meaning, you've made everyone feel welcome—your guests feel like "family." This is okay. It's complimentary.

So welcome those who drop by, if it's convenient. It can be both fun and flattering to reminisce about a party you've just had with a satisfied guest. If it's a bad time, let the drop-by know this and thank them for stopping in.

# the last word

The last word on your parties is always yours. Be positive. Never, not under any circumstances, complain about how much work a party was. Never talk about how "crazy" the evening was, don't mention how hard the main course was to make, or how hard it was or how much money it took to get the band to play for a few extra hours. Don't talk about costs.

Don't speak negatively about a guest. Not even if they behaved poorly or did something terribly embarrassing. Don't be too positive, either. Don't count heads, estimate guests or "brag" about your party in any way. Don't call your party "the event of the year" (even if other people do). Don't be self-congratulating. Nana Malloy always used to say, "Don't believe your own P.R.," while Grandpa Kucera says, "The empty wagon always makes the most noise." Let other people do the talking about your parties if they choose.

Do thank people when they compliment you on your party. Then thank them for coming. After all, they were the ones that truly "made" the event.

Do tell people that you had a wonderful time, that your guests were fabulous, that everyone seemed to have fun, and that you can't wait to do it again soon.

# elements

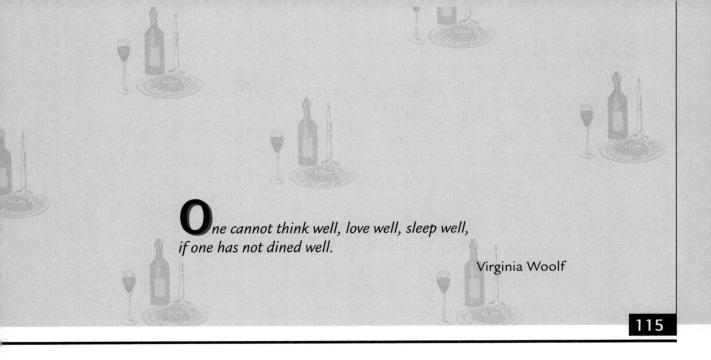

*One cannot think well, love well, sleep well,
if one has not dined well.*

Virginia Woolf

# food

## cookbooks

The following cookbooks offer classic, basic recipes, and are well written and easy to follow. Of course, you don't need to own all of them, but if you can, you should own one of them. These folks are the experts.

*The Way to Cook* and *Julia's Kitchen Wisdom*
Julia Child

*Joy of Cooking*
Irma S. Rombauer

*The New York Times Cookbook*
Craig Claiborne

*How to Cook Everything*
Mark Bittman

## U.S. weights & measures

3 teaspoons = 1 tablespoon = ½ ounce (liquid and dry)
2 tablespoons = 1 ounce (liquid and dry)
4 tablespoons = 2 ounces (liquid and dry) = ¼ cup
16 tablespoons = 8 ounces = 1 cup = ½ pound
16 tablespoons = 48 teaspoons
32 tablespoons = 16 ounces = 2 cups = 1 pound
64 tablespoons = 32 ounces = 1 quart = 2 pounds
1 cup = 8 ounces (liquid) = ½ pint
2 cups = 16 ounces (liquid) = 1 pint
4 cups = 32 ounces (liquid) = 2 pints = 1 quart
16 cups = 128 ounces (liquid) = 4 quarts = 1 gallon
1 quart = 2 pints (dry)

# the basic pantry

While it seems like a lot to look at, once you have the
following items, you're ready to tackle most anything. All you'll
need are your fresh ingredients, and you're ready to cook. You
probably have many of these items already, but if you don't,
there's no need to rush out and buy all of them at once. As
you cook more often, you'll build up your stock.

### dry herbs & spices

| | | |
|---|---|---|
| Allspice | Fennel Seeds | Pepper: Dried Red |
| Basil | Ginger | Peppercorns (Black) |
| Bay Leaves | Mace | Rosemary |
| Celery Seeds | Marjoram | Sage |
| Chili Powder | Mint | Salt: Kosher |
| Cinnamon | Mustard Seed | Salt: Table |
| Cloves | Nutmeg | Salt: Sea |
| Cumin | Oregano | Sesame Seeds |
| Curry Powder | Paprika | Tarragon |
| Dill | Pepper: Cayenne | Thyme |

### basics—nonrefrigerated

| | | |
|---|---|---|
| Baking Powder | Extracts | Soy Sauce |
| Baking Soda | Flours | Sugars |
| Beans | Honey | Syrups |
| Bouillon | Horseradish | Tabasco Sauce |
| Bread Crumbs | Ketchup | Teas |
| Broths | Mustards | Teriyaki Sauce |
| Capers | Nuts | Tomatoes (canned, several types) |
| Chocolate | Oils | |
| Clam Juice | Olives | Vinegars |
| Cocoa | Pastas | Wines (for cooking) |
| Coffee | Pickles | Worcestershire Sauce |
| Cornstarch | Preserves | Yeast |
| Cream of Tartar | Rice | |

*basics—refrigerated*

| | |
|---|---|
| Butter (unsalted) | Eggs |
| Cheeses | Mayonnaise |
| Creams | Milk |

# entertaining basics
## (things to have on hand
### in case of drop-by guests)

Baguette or other bread

Beer

Bottled Water (with and without bubbles)

Coffee

Cheeses

Cookies

Crackers

Liquor (a selection)

Milk

Nuts

Olives

Seltzer

Soda (diet and regular)

Tonic

Wine

# stuff

From what you can tell by catalogs and magazines and, especially if you've ever registered for a wedding (or perused someone else's bridal registry)—you need approximately 457 kitchen items to make cereal.

Truth be told, you don't need four different mixers, twenty different pans, fourteen pots and an assortment of matching dishtowels in order to cook. You do, however, need the basics. You should spend within your budget but keep in mind that investing in a few good pots, pans and knives can be smart. Good nonstick pans, for instance, speed cooking and cleanup and last for years. And sharp knives, while hazardous to klutzes like Julie, are indispensable in the kitchen. What we suggest is to own fewer pieces—but good quality. Here's what we'd suggest you own.

- 1 large nonstick frying pan and 1 smaller nonstick frying pan
- 1 large iron skillet with a cover
- 1 large covered stockpot
- 2 sauce pans, 1 small and one large
- 1 large roasting pan
- 2 nonstick cookie sheets
- 2 (different sized) glass baking dishes
- 1 colander
- 1 blender and 1 hand mixer

- A few cutting boards (some plastic, some wood— have a big one for meats)
- 1 good pair of kitchen scissors
- Some wooden spoons, whisks, metal and rubber spatulas, slotted spoons and the like, a can opener, a peeler, a garlic press, a bottle opener, a grater, a rolling pin, tongs, a thermometer, kitchen towels, an oven mitt and whatever else you like to use
- Glass mixing bowls in assorted sizes and a few stainless steel mixing bowls
- Measuring cups and spoons, and a glass (2C or larger) liquid measuring cup
- A pepper mill
- A good set of very sharp knives, and a sharpener

There are many other things you can buy. But don't clutter up your kitchen too much, and remember, you probably don't really need much "stuff" to get a good meal on the table.

For instance, we've entertained for years without a citrus zester, a nutmeg grater or even (horrors) a food processor.

# why you really love your mail carrier

The following stores can deliver foods and specialty ingredients throughout the United States and right to your home. Just remember to order with enough time for shipping, so the goods arrive before your party. Please note that the telephone numbers and web sites are valid as of the date of publication. There are many other fine establishments that offer delivery. Call them—you'll be surprised what you can get with a push-button phone.

Citarella (212) 874-0383

One of New York City's best fine food shops, online. Offers a number of prepared foods.

*www.citarella.com*

Dean & DeLuca (877) 826-9246

This is a classic gourmet shop online, with outstanding quality and presentation.

*www.deandeluca.com*

Harrington's of Vermont (802) 434-4444

Known for their hams—very useful for large parties or brunches.

*www.harringtonham.com*

Williams-Sonoma (877) 812-6235

Williams-Sonoma is a known entity (you know the quality) and offers some good basics.

*www.williams-sonoma.com*

# in a pinch . . .

The following recipes are super easy and very satisfying—great "fall back" recipes for the times when you're looking forward to seeing your guests but not the cooking, and take-out just doesn't seem right. We use these recipes all the time and haven't heard a complaint yet. Enjoy!

## fondue

No, you don't need to wear "love beads" or peace sign necklaces to enjoy fondue. Fondue is a terrific way to entertain. It involves everyone, invites conversation and is economical and easy. If you can find a good cheese shop, you'll be better off. We use the Darien Cheese Shop in Darien, Connecticut, and they even grate and dredge our cheese for us (we love them). Otherwise:

1  Have enough fondue pots. Don't make people stand up or reach too far to get to the fondues.
2  Don't serve cold beverages—rumor has it that the cheese will ball up in the stomach and give your guests a stomachache. Room temperature water or red wine is okay.
3  Each guest should have a plate and a fondue fork (along with a napkin and beverage).

4 Steak fondue is nice to have with cheese fondue (it adds variety). Slice steak thin and heat peanut oil for frying in a fondue pot. Guests fry the steak themselves.

The following recipe serves 4 as a main course or 8–12 otherwise.

1 clove garlic
1½ cups dry white wine
1 tablespoon lemon juice (fresh)
1 pound mix of Emmentaler and Swiss cheeses, grated and dredged in 1 tablespoon flour
crusty Italian or French bread, cubed

On stovetop, rub inside of fondue pot with cut garlic clove. Pour wine into pot and add lemon juice. Heat over medium flame until wine is hot but not boiling. Add handfuls of cheese, stirring constantly until cheese is melted and the cheese-wine mixture has the appearance of a light creamy sauce. Bring to a boil, then remove pot and place on fondue stand with lighted burner underneath. Keep burner on so that the fondue continues to bubble lightly. Serve each guest bread cubes and let them spear the bread and dip into the fondue.

Serve a LOT of red wine, let your hair down and have fun.

# additional fondue sauces
## and variations

If simple cheese and steak fondues sound a bit boring, don't be afraid to spice things up. Be creative!

## fondue seasonings

Standard cheese fondue seasonings include freshly ground pepper, nutmeg and paprika. Feel free to go crazy, though. Let loose: try popping in some dill, tarragon or rosemary. Toss in some mushrooms if you feel game. Or, if you're feeling especially frisky, pour in some liquor like bourbon, rum or brandy. (Just don't go overboard or the seasoning will quickly overpower or compete with the cheese.)

## dipping sauces

We don't often use dipping sauces with our steak fondue, but many people do, and if you're looking for some extra flavor, this is a good place to add it. A steak sauce we love and use often is a basic horseradish sauce (in fact you'll see it again in this book—with our fillet of beef recipe). It couldn't be easier to whip up.

# horseradish sauce

Whip whipping cream (amount depends on your party) until fluffy.

Fold prepared horseradish and a pinch or two of salt into the whipped cream until tangy, to taste.

Or, try the following all-purpose dipping sauces. Just combine the ingredients in each recipe.

### all-purpose dipping sauce
$1/2$ cup soy sauce

1 teaspoon sesame oil

$1/2$ cup rice vinegar

### mustard sauce
$1/2$ cup Dijon mustard (we use Maille Dijon Originale for everything with Dijon)

$1/4$ cup dry white wine

Whatever sauce you decide to serve, serve it in a gravy boat or separate bowl with a spoon, so your guests can put some on their plate if they so choose. Even better, put tiny bowls of sauces at each place.

# fondue for dessert

Fondue for dessert is extremely simple and always goes over well. Change locations (move everyone out onto a patio or into your living room) and serve with a nice bottle of Port.

# chocolate fondue

This makes 6 to 8 servings:

6 1-oz. squares unsweetened chocolate
1½ cups sugar
½ cup butter
1 cup light cream
1 pinch salt
3 tablespoons flavored liqueur (like Chambord)—completely optional

In a saucepan melt chocolate over low heat. Add sugar, cream, butter and salt. Cook, stirring constantly, about 5 minutes or until thickened. Stir in liqueur if you're using it. Pour into fondue pot and place over burner to keep warm.

Serve chocolate fondue with an assortment of fruits (like strawberries, cubed melons, sliced bananas or cubed pineapples). Just be sure the fruits are sturdy and not slippery (or else they'll break apart or fall off the fondue fork). Also nice is cubed pieces of pound cake, but it's fairly heavy.

# antipasto

Antipasto can be a hearty first course or a whole meal. And just about all of it can be bought in a good Italian grocery or in the deli section of a decent grocery store. Simply set the following items out—arrange on a large white platter or on several smaller platters and bowls (for a buffet).

Serve with plenty of wine, a nice sorbet for dessert, and you've got yourself a fantastic summer meal.

- A variety of olives
- Salami
- Soppressata
- Fresh mozzarella
- Roasted peppers
- Fresh provolone
- A wedge of Parmigiano-Reggiano
- Prosciutto
- Marinated artichoke hearts
- Marinated mushrooms
- Several loaves of Italian bread
- Herbed olive oil

# pizza

On a day-to-day basis, we can't think of anything we enjoy eating more than pizza. Who doesn't love a slice? Good pizza is right up there with good french fries as "must haves" in life. We truly believe that anything you love, your guests will probably enjoy —even if only as a result of your heartfelt enthusiasm.

We think pizza is a fun thing to make for small groups of people for dinner. We say small groups only because unless you have several large ovens, you can't make very many pizzas at a time.

Tips on making pizza:

- Get a pizza stone. Williams-Sonoma carries them, and while they seem superfluous (Julie busted Ron's chops for registering for one, and now she's eating her words—literally), they really do improve and speed up pizza cooking.
- Buy your pizza dough ready-made and fresh. Most pizza places sell their dough for around $1.00 for a large pie-sized ball and many grocery stores sell it fresh in their deli department (for about the same price). Buying it ready made is a lot easier than waiting for dough to rise. And your time is definitely worth a buck, right?

- Use cornmeal instead of flour to keep the dough from sticking.
- Use high quality ingredients. We like to use Rao's Homemade Marinara Sauce as our pizza sauce, but if you can't get that, just buy something good. Just because it's pizza (and the dough only set you back a few dollars), don't skimp where it counts. Use good shredded mozzarella. Add some freshly grated Parmesan as well—this really perks up a pie.
- Be creative. We like to serve an assortment. Try:

  Pesto with grilled chicken, pine nuts and a light dusting of Parmesan

  Tomato sauce (like Rao's), hot sausage, onions, mozzarella and Parmesan

  Gorgonzola cheese and walnuts drizzled with olive oil

Serve your pizzas with a nice balsamic vinaigrette salad, several bottles of Pinot Grigio, and ice cream for dessert. Everyone will be happy. You can't miss.

# cheese course

Sure, it's high in fat, but you only live once . . . and what's a life without cheese? Boring. So lighten up, slim, and bring on the Brie.

Cheese courses are extremely easy to put together (there's nothing real hard about buying cheese, a few nice baguettes and some crackers)—and they can be fun, different and satisfying. They can be served before dessert or as dessert, depending on what you serve as a main course.

If you serve a very heavy or rich main course, you should probably omit the dessert if you want to serve cheese after dinner, especially since it's not nice to cause clogged arteries. In either case, open up a nice tawny Port, put out the cheese and breads, and party on.

Selecting cheeses for the cheese course and serving it is not too tricky, but here are a few pointers, and a list of good cheeses to try. The best tip you'll ever get from us is: find a good local cheese source.

We have a fantastic local cheese shop that we use relentlessly when we entertain. They give us suggestions on new cheeses and patés to try, they advise us about compatibility, and they let us know how best to serve each item. Try to find a similar source, even if it simply means getting to know the manager of the cheese department in your grocery store. If you can't find a good local source, drive or ride the phone. We can't emphasize enough how important cheese and a good cheese source are to living a happy, full life.

- Try to balance the cheeses with the rest of the meal (more extravagant cheeses with a light meal, or simpler, lighter cheeses with a heavy, rich meal).
- Try to have contrasts in your selection: a few hard cheeses, a few soft, a few exotic and one or two that people will recognize.
- Two ounces of cheese per person is probably enough.
- Cheese should always be served room temperature—never cold.
- Fresh fruit is a nice accompaniment, but not necessary. A few suggestions: strawberries (whole or sliced), raspberries, blueberries, blackberries and cherries.
- Serve with thinly sliced French baguette slices, or nonflavored crackers.

Save the Velveeta for your furry friends, and serve the following cheeses to your guests.

### *Hard*

Dry Jack
Parmigiano-Reggiano
Pepato

### Semifirm
Cheddar

Gruyere

### Blues
Saga Blue

Stilton

### Chevres
Boucheron

Montrachet

### Semisoft
Fontina

Morbier

Port-Salut

### Soft
Brie

Camembert

L'Explorateur

St. Andre

# cheese and wine compatibility

While wine and cheese compatibility largely depends on taste (yours, not ours), there are a few guidelines that can start you off in a reasonable direction.

- If you are choosing to serve several cheeses together, a medium-bodied red wine like a Merlot works best.
- We serve Champagne with Brie or a triple crème cheese. Champagne and rich, creamy cheeses is lovely and classic.

If you are serving just one type of cheese, the following applies:

- With goat cheeses, serve a light, fruity white wine like Sauvignon Blanc, Chenin Blanc or the sweet Gewürztraminer.
- With creamy or strong cheeses like blue, red wines work best. Try something a bit sweet, like a Zinfandel or Merlot.
- We personally like to serve tawny Port with a selection of cheeses, if we're serving them at the end of the evening in lieu of dessert.

# reality check

### keeping cheese fresh

- Store cheese in the produce or dairy drawer in your fridge.
- Wrap it in airtight plastic or aluminum foil, and change the wrap when you use it.

- If mold appears on your cheese, it's harmless. Just scrape it off with a knife.
- If you notice your cheeses molding quickly, wrap them less tightly, to allow for air.

# "the regulars"

Over the years, we've served many different foods incorporated into a variety of menus; most worked, some didn't. Since you probably wouldn't appreciate our sharing our worst meal attempts with you (one tip: despite what anybody—even a butcher—may tell you, do NOT wrap fillets of beef in tin foil to cook . . . very unappetizing results), you'll find some of our favorite recipes, or our "regulars" (including one for a beef fillet—sans tin foil, of course) here.

We've included our Fourth of July party menu because it's a good example of a simple, crowd-pleasing menu that is perfect for large casual gatherings.

We've also included recipes for a few other dishes we're fond of serving. They range from beef to seafood, none of them are too difficult to master, and none take too much time or any special equipment to make. Enjoy!

# ron and julie's
# fourth of july party menu

Our Fourth of July party is a big (we plan for 300 people), crowded, casual event that includes all of our favorite people, from our elderly friends to the children of our peers. It begins around 5:00 P.M. and inevitably ends early in the morning the next day. This is a lot of people to feed over a long period of time, so the menu is pretty basic, hassle-free, and safe (no mayonnaise-based salads, no poultry, no fish).

Here's what we generally serve:

High quality (butcher shop) hamburgers and hot dogs
Fresh buns from a bakery (be sure to ask them to slice the buns—we once forgot, huge mistake)
Fresh cole slaw (recipe on page 139)
Ron's "hunting" baked beans (recipe on page 140)
Ice cream sandwiches (store bought)

As you can see, this is a very basic, no fuss menu, but nobody leaves hungry and everyone has a wonderful time.

We also put out simple, all-American snack foods as well, like pretzels, chips and nuts (again, nothing that spoils in the sun, heat or humidity).

Okay, we'll admit it: we also serve a roast pig.

Roasting a pig outdoors is a festive thing to do and many people love it. We rent a rotisserie and put it in an out-of-the-way, down-wind location (it puts out a lot of smoke), and our friend Mike provides us with a fennel- and apple-stuffed pig. Minding and carving the pig is a lot of work, so we hire someone.

138

Words of caution: if you decide to serve roast pig, be aware that many people do not like it (or even the sight of it), so put it in an avoidable place (not the center of your party) and offer plenty of other foods. In fact, we serve the whole menu with the pig as a side dish, for those who like or want to try it.

One more thing! About those condiments . . . for even the most casual gatherings, don't plop catsup, mustard, salsa or pickle relish containers on the table. Bowls, gravy boats or even generic plastic squeeze bottles (all available at many grocery stores, kitchen stores like Williams-Sonoma and Crate and Barrel, or restaurant supply stores) make much nicer condiment servers than the original containers. Make it look like you're putting forth some kind of effort for your guests, and spare them from having to look at the price tag on your pickles.

# "it'll last as long as you do," no-mayonnaise cole slaw

We scale this recipe way up to suit our needs. It's fairly messy to make and shredding the cabbage is kind of a pain, but it can be made ahead of time (just don't combine the dressing and the cabbage until the day of the party), people love it, and it doesn't go bad quickly.

Serves 6 to 8

½ cup apple cider vinegar

2 tablespoons Dijon mustard

1 tablespoon honey

1½ cups vegetable oil

1 head green cabbage, shredded

1 head red cabbage, shredded

1½ teaspoons celery seed

Salt and freshly ground pepper to taste

Combine the vinegar, mustard, oil, celery seed and honey in a bowl and stir. Add the cabbage and stir. Season with salt and pepper to taste.

# ron's hunting baked beans

When Ron goes hunting in Texas, they pretty much subsist on candy, Sangria and smoked meat. While to the sober, non-hunting-on-a-ranch-in-Texas-for-a-week rest of us, this may sound pretty gross, we can vouch for one thing: these guys clearly know how to make baked beans. Their "recipe" has since found its shining glory on the buffet table at our Yankee Fourth of July party.

There's no need to be exact here, folks. The boys in Texas make this after a full day of hunting and Sangria drinking, and it comes out just fine.

140

Canned baked beans
A decent prepared barbecue sauce
Bacon (uncooked, plenty of it)
Jack Daniels or Makers Mark

Pour the baked beans into either an aluminum roasting pan or a large stockpot (depending on how much you're making). Stir in some barbecue sauce and a splash or two of liquor. Top with strips of uncooked bacon (pre-cook the bacon if using a stockpot. In either case, if you're feeling energetic, you can cut the bacon into inch-wide pieces.) Heat the beans, either on the stovetop (in the stockpot) or in the oven (with the roasting pan) at a medium to low-level heat, until the bacon is cooked through. If you cut the bacon, stir it in, or if it's in strips, remove it before serving. Serve in a large bowl or chafing dish.

# other recipes

These are some of our other standbys . . .

# rosemary and garlic pork chops

These pork chops are simple and tasty, can be grilled or cooked in the kitchen, and are crowd-pleasing. Please note that for this recipe, you could easily substitute chicken breasts (bone in) for the pork chops, and it would be lovely. As with many of our recipes, the amounts depend on the number of guests you're serving, so you need to adjust accordingly. The marinade is to taste and should be enough to pour over the chops so they're sitting in it. Unless you make so much marinade the chops are covered (which isn't really necessary), you should turn them once while they marinade.

Center cut pork chops, bone in.

Marinade:

Mix together, in a food processor (if you have one—otherwise, mash the garlic and rosemary together with a mortar and pestle, then combine with other ingredients in a separate bowl):

Olive oil
Freshly pressed garlic cloves
Fresh or dried rosemary
Coarse sea salt and pepper

Pour marinade over the chops and let them marinade, turning once, for a few hours.

Preheat the oven to 350°.

In a heavy skillet, pour in a few tablespoons of olive oil and heat, on medium-high, until the skillet and the oil are hot. Put the chops in the skillet and brown them on both sides. This takes a few minutes on each side.

Once browned, transfer the chops onto a roasting pan and put them in the preheated oven. Check for doneness in about 20 minutes. Chops should be cooked through.

(You can also grill the pork chops.)

# grilled whole red snapper

Serving a whole fish can be dramatic and fun, and it's easier than it sounds. Be careful when grilling whole fish, however, since the skin is likely to fall off, and you want to be sure the meat stays on the bone. If you would rather not deal with that, you can always broil. Serves 4.

1 whole red snapper, cleaned (gilled, gutted and scaled—have your fish market do this—leave the head and tail on)
Coarse sea salt and freshly ground pepper
Lemon wedges

Heat the grill or oven to medium-hot.

Salt and pepper the fish to taste. Place the fish on a grill rack (or fish grilling basket). If you're broiling, oil the broiling pan before putting the fish on it.

Grill or broil the fish for about 5 minutes per side. Check for doneness along the central bone with a thin, sharp knife; done fish will be white and flaky.

Serve with lemon wedges.

# beef fillet with horseradish sauce

Another dish we serve year-round, this is a great dish to make for a large crowd and can be formal without being difficult. All you have to do is pop a fillet in the oven, and make a simple sauce. (Note: The simple potato dish and salad that follow go beautifully with this dish.) This recipe serves 6 to 8.

1 3-pound fillet of beef
Olive oil
Freshly ground black pepper
Salt

Preheat the oven to 450°. Lightly oil, salt and pepper the fillet. Oil the roasting pan as well. Put the fillet on a roasting pan and cook for approximately 20 minutes for a rare fillet.

Slice thinly (about ¼″ thick) and serve with the following horseradish sauce.

# horseradish sauce

Whip whipping cream until fluffy.

Fold prepared horseradish and a pinch or two of salt into the whipped cream until tangy, to taste.

# rosemary roasted potatoes

If you want to make your guests (those who aren't on low-carb diets) really happy, serve these potatoes! This is a personal favorite of ours. It works well for buffets, since it can be made ahead of time and reheated with little consequence, and tastes just fine room temperature.

New potatoes, cut into bite-size pieces
Fresh rosemary
Olive oil—enough to simply coat the potatoes
Kosher salt
Pepper

Preheat your oven to 350°.

In a large Ziploc bag, combine the potatoes, olive oil, rosemary, salt and pepper. Shake vigorously until potatoes are evenly coated. Lightly coat a baking sheet with olive oil, put the potatoes on the baking sheet in one layer, and bake for approximately 45 minutes.

# gorgonzola and
## toasted walnut salad

This salad is extremely pleasing, even to people who don't really like salad (the added benefits of nuts and cheese are a big draw).

This is especially nice in the fall and winter months, but in warmer weather, just omit the Dijon mustard from the dressing and add sliced pears (soaked in lemon so they don't brown).

Mesclun lettuce salad, clean and dry
Gorgonzola cheese, crumbled
Walnuts, chopped and toasted*
Basic Dijon vinaigrette (see following)

In a large salad bowl, combine the lettuce, cheese and toasted walnuts. Pour on enough dressing to coat (try not to overdress), and toss well.

Basic Dijon Vinaigrette
Whisk together:
1 cup olive oil
4 tablespoons white wine vinegar
2 tablespoons lemon juice
2 tablespoons Dijon mustard
1 garlic clove, pressed
Coarse sea salt and ground pepper, to taste

* The easiest way to toast nuts is to put them on tin foil or a baking sheet and put them in either the oven or a toaster oven at about 400° for a few minutes (most likely, around 5). Check them every few minutes, moving them around a bit so they cook evenly and don't burn.

# tricky food (and how to eat it)

We have all been faced with certain peculiar foods that we simply don't know what on earth they are, let alone what to do with them. And other times we know what the food is, maybe we even eat it at home all the time, but we're not sure how to eat it properly in front of company.

Staring at these foods doesn't work, nor does trying to cover them with a side dish. You're going to have to jump on that grenade.

We know, we know: you're asking, "Why on earth would I serve something I don't know how to eat?" Certainly, most of the time you wouldn't. Occasionally, however, when you work with a caterer (and you don't sample food ahead of time), or if you entertain at a restaurant or club, you might run into the random dish that you have no idea how to eat properly.

Your guests will look to you as an example of how to eat what you're serving. Here's how to eat several typically perplexing things.

## artichokes

Eat artichokes with your fingers, from the outside leaves in, one leaf at a time. Dip the base of the leaf (where the meaty, edible portion can be found) in any available sauce, slide it between your teeth and pull it forward, eating the "meat." Place the rest of the leaf on the side of your plate. When you have finished eating all of the leaves and have reached the center of the artichoke, scrape away the fuzzy portion (choke) with a knife. Place the fuzz on your plate next to the leaves. What remains is the heart. Cut it into bitesize portions with a fork and knife.

## asparagus

Eat with a knife and fork in formal situations. It can be eaten with the fingers in casual settings, unless it is limp or has a sauce, which would make it very messy to pick up. Use your best judgment.

## bread and butter

Break the bread into manageable pieces with your fingers. Using a clean butter knife (or whatever knife you do have), put the butter on your plate, then butter your bread, one piece at a time.

## caviar

Use the spoon it is served with to put the caviar on your plate. Transfer the caviar from your plate onto toasts, using your own knife or spoon, and if other condiments are served, serve yourself accordingly, placing these items on top of the caviar on the toast.

## clams, mussels, oysters

Hold the shell in one hand and the shellfish fork in your other. Spear the meat with the fork, dip it into the sauce, and eat it in one bite. If it sticks to the shell in this process, use your fork to pry it loose. If you're at a casual bar or restaurant (that doesn't provide the forks), it is okay to suck the meat down directly from the shell, despite the fact that while writing this, that sounds disgusting.

## lobster

When serving, it is nice to crack lobster shells before serving them so your guests don't have to use all of their power to open them. Then provide guests with nutcrackers or shellfish crackers to finish the job, and have a receptacle for discarding shells throughout the meal. Have lots of napkins, since this gets messy. You can put a bowl of water with lemon juice in it at each place for cleaning hands.

When eating, crack slowly so you don't make a big mess and splatter the person next to you with the highly unbecoming scent of lobster juice.

Crack the claws—first twist them off the body—then crack each claw and pull out the meat with a fork or your fingers. For the tail, pull the meat out with your fork in long strips, then cut up into bite-size pieces. The red roe and green "fat" are edible, and many people like them.

If you are inclined, you can break off the legs, put them in your mouth (okay, one at a time), bite down and suck out the meat. Try to resist acting like a vampire.

## snails (escargots)

Sure they look funny. You would too if you spent your life sucking on a rock in the ocean. Clamp the snail with provided utensil (there are specific snail utensils available—provide these if you're planning to serve snails). If there are no utensils, use your fingers to hold the snail. With the other hand, get the meat out of the shell with a shellfish fork, and eat.

## spaghetti and other pasta

Just be neat, okay? If the pasta is stringy, you can twirl the pasta around on your fork, with the fork pressed against your plate or against a large spoon. Or you can cut the pasta into manageable pieces. Try very hard not to have dangling pasta or to bite it midway so that a big portion of it drops back into your plate. Sometimes it can't be helped, though, and most everyone understands.

## sushi or sashimi

The neatest way to eat this is whole, but that makes many people gag.

If you're using your fingers (generally you'd only do this with sushi), you can easily bite the piece in half. This is a lot harder to do when using chopsticks, unless you're very dexterous. Usually it ends with a piece of half-bitten sushi dangling from your mouth, which is pretty hard to recover from socially, but doable.

If you are being served sushi or sashimi from a platter, and you are using chopsticks, use the fat end of the chopsticks to pick up the pieces (since it won't have been stuck in your mouth, thank you).

152

*A woman drove me to drink, and I didn't have the decency to thank her.*

W. C. Fields

*Drink to me.*

Pablo Picasso's last words

# drinks

## self-serve bar basics

If you offer the following at your self-serve bar, you are giving your guests a fairly complete selection. Few guests expect you to offer the selection of a bar or restaurant; as a matter of fact, many guests don't expect much more than beer, wine, and some nonalcoholic offerings (but they're your guests, so we suggest you lay it out there).

Depending on your party, you can downsize or add to this list.

- Champagne
- Beer
- White wines
- Red wines
- Rosé
- Gin
- Scotch
- Rum
- Whiskey
- An aperitif

- Seltzer, sparkling water
- Sodas—diet and regular
- Ginger Ale
- Juices—orange, tomato, cranberry
- Mixers (tonic, club soda, etc.)
- Vodka
- Lemons, limes, olives
- Lots of ice—and a cooler
- Bar tools (corkscrew, knife, shaker)
- Cocktail napkins and a bar towel
- More ice

154

# bar location

Don't have a buffet and a bar next to one another; it's a sure way to create a major bottleneck. People go to the buffet, but they hang out at the bar. Separate them. If possible, set up two bars, one on either end of the party.

Avoid setting up your bar in a congested location (near a corner, in a narrow hallway). Similarly, don't set it up too far out of the way; since so many people linger there, you'll divide your party. Try to set the bar up in a slightly out-of-the-way or off-to-one-side location, where everyone can see and get to it, people can linger around it shortly, but where nobody will be excluded from the party while there.

If using help, be sure to provide room for them to work behind the bar, as well as space for storage. Also consider the fact that people will gather around the bar, so be sure there's adequate space for them to mingle. If you've set up a self-serve bar, be sure it's fully accessible.

*Do not allow children to mix drinks. It is unseemly, and they use too much vermouth.*

Steve Allen

# setting up the bar

If you have any precious surfaces near the bar (the table, flooring), protect them with plastic sheeting (a cut open trash bag will work) and then cover or hide the plastic with a tablecloth. Chill beverages that need it ahead of time. To save time when serving later, open wines and put the corks back in the bottles loosely, then chill.

You will need twice as many glasses as guests (at least) because people misplace them.

## chilling

Have you ever had a run on white wine and found that the only bottles in your possession were in a cabinet, warm? This will get you out of that jam.

Immerse the item to be chilled in a bucket full of ice and cold water. The combination of ice and cold water works much more efficiently than straight ice (yet it still takes over half an hour to chill a warm bottle of Champagne, so give everything time). For chilling large quantities of bottles, large tin buckets are ideal. In a pinch, however, a large and very, very clean trash bin works perfectly. Fill with ice, water from the hose and your warm beverages.

Note: When chilling this way, labels begin to fall off. Be sure you don't soak the bottles too long in water, or this gets messy.

# a word about kegs

Kegs can be very convenient, but we know more than one host who served warm beer because—horrors of all frat boy horrors!—he didn't properly prepare the keg.

Okay. College was a few years back, so listen up: keep your keg chilled. If you pick it up cold, put it in a container filled with ice and topped with ice blocks. Keep it in the shade, or cover it with a light-colored tarp. If you pick it up warm and have to chill it, put it in a container and fill the container up with cold water and ice, then cover.

No container? No problem. Most liquor stores (where you'll get the keg) rent keg containers. At the very least, they'll give you a keg bag (a beefed-up trash bag), which will do the trick.

Chilling a keg takes a long time, so don't start this process two hours before the party and expect a nice frosty beer to come pouring out of the tap. Set aside at least a day (morning until an evening party) for full chilling.

If you have any further questions, please consult any friends or relatives still in college. Or someone very manly.

Thank you.

# glasses

Only spend a fortune on your crystal if you've got the money to lose. It will break. So buy affordable, yet elegant, stemware— and relax. Buy stemware that can be replaced (you'll need to), and accept that you might need to mix stemware styles to accommodate all of your guests. It's just a part of life. In a nutshell: buy what you like, but figure it's going to break soon.

A few basics:

- A wineglass should have a stem, so that you can hold the glass without warming the wine.
- For red wines, the glass should be bigger and taper in toward the top.
- White wineglasses are often smaller than red wineglasses, but both should be sized large enough to allow the wines to breathe.

- Fluted Champagne glasses are preferable to the bowl-type, but if you have the bowls, use them, especially if you serve a Champagne punch.
- Lowball glasses and highball glasses should be heavy enough to feel sturdy and strong and, basically, masculine.

## bring it on!

Having guests bring their own bottles is acceptable for casual get-togethers, like picnics and family-oriented parties.

# reality check

### serving wine

- For both red and white wines, don't pour a full glass—you need to allow the wine room to breathe in the bowl.
- Pour enough into the glass to be generous, but don't fill the glass.

- We like to pour until the glass curves inwards (stopping at the widest part of the glass), but this depends on your stemware and your preference.

However, if you should choose to do this, remember a few things first.

- As host, you are responsible for having a bare minimum of beverages for your guests. Have at least enough for all guests to have three drinks without anyone bringing anything.
- Don't forget that you will need to chill white wines and beers, so make plans accordingly. Have a large container for ice and water, or have a spare fridge set up for chilling (if you have one).

## reality check

### the problematic punch bowl

Serving alcohol-laden punch at large parties can certainly make things more interesting.

That said, if you plan on doing this and having children at the party (and you don't plan on having a bartender overseeing the punch at all times), you need to be careful.

- Be sure you label the punch container, indicating "no children" or "adults only," so kids don't drink the spiked punch.
- And tell the parents that the punch is spiked, in case the label falls off, gets lost, or the kids can't read yet.
- Also, have a smaller container with—and this is important—a different colored punch—for the kids.

- Be sure to ask for an array of beverages, so that there is a selection for your guests.
- Don't ask guests to bring their preferred beverage. You don't want guests upset because another guest drank the wine they brought. Just ask guests to bring a certain type of beverage, and leave it at that.
- Remember to have people bring (or provide yourself) nonalcoholic beverages.
- Remember to provide lots of ice.
- Bottom line: if you run out, remember that the thirsty guests are at your house. Be sure you're covered.

# our favorite drinks

Good drinks are like good dogs—trustworthy and dependable.

Aside from beer, wine and a standard bar, we have a few favorite mixed drinks that we serve regularly to our guests. As a host, one should try to develop a stable of basic mixed drinks. These will consist of beverages you serve for small gatherings (frozen margaritas—we learned the lesson—are not easy to serve to lots of people), and beverages you can serve to big crowds (one word: sangria).

We have a few basic mixed drinks in our stable. Of course, sometimes we serve others, but these are our favorites. Herein, we're providing you with the recipes for these drinks. We hope these drinks help make your parties more memorable . . . as they do ours. Bottoms up!

*Always do sober what you said you'd do drunk.*
*That will teach you to keep your mouth shut.*

Ernest Hemingway

# russ's margaritas

Our friend Russ makes amazing margaritas that have set us back on more than one occasion. Behold the secret recipe below. Remember, you can serve margaritas any time. They're actually a great drink to serve if people are stopping by for "just a drink" (before going out to dinner, or in the afternoon, or for breakfast (kidding). . .). As you can see, they're easy to make (no need for a blender).

The following recipe makes several.

3/4 can Limeade
4 shots Tequila
2 shots Triple Sec
Juice of 1 lime
Salt
Beer—about 2 swigs—to cut the "tart"
Crushed ice

Mix everything except the salt and crushed ice. Salt the rim of each glass and pour margarita mixture over crushed ice. Serve to good friends and have fun.

*One more drink and I'd be under the host.*

Dorothy Parker

# mojitos

Mojitos are a great way to loosen up a crowd. (We learned this trick at Julie's brother Jeff's rehearsal dinner in Miami.) Serve them when guests arrive and be prepared to keep 'em coming—people love them. Be warned, though: Mojitos are very strong and go down plenty easy. As our friend Eduardo would say, "Let me tell you something . . ." about Mojitos: we've had them in Miami, we've had them in Paris, and wherever you drink Mojitos, there's a party.

Serves 10

3$1/2$ cups light rum

1$1/4$ cups fresh lime juice (this has to be fresh squeezed)

$1/3$ cup of sugar syrup (recipe follows)

Soda water

Ice cubes for serving

Wedges of lime

Sprigs of mint

Stir the rum, lime juice and sugar syrup together. Put ice in glass, pour rum mixture over ice, top off with soda water and garnish with lime wedge and mint sprig.

## simple syrup

Mix 1 cup of water with 3 cups of sugar; boil for 5 minutes, bottle and refrigerate.

*Work is the curse of the drinking class.*

Oscar Wilde

# mrs. underwood's mint juleps

We were "Mint Julep Virgins" when we arrived at the Underwood's house in Louisville for the Kentucky Derby. When we left, we were full-blown addicts. Mrs. Underwood's mint juleps are impossible to refuse—and while this has a lot to do with her significant charms, the juleps are just darn good. She very graciously agreed to share her family recipe with you all when we asked her.

- Fill a jar loosely with sprigs of fresh mint. Don't crush the mint! If crushed, you could embarrass a beautiful Derby guest in her "to die for Derby hat" as she smiles with a large piece of green mint in her front teeth! Cover the mint with 2 cups simple syrup. Cap and refrigerate 12–24 hours. Discard mint.

- Make one julep at a time: Fill a chilled, preferably silver, julep cup with finely crushed ice, pour in half a tablespoon of the mint-flavored syrup and 2 ounces of the very best Kentucky Bourbon (we prefer Maker's Mark). Frost cup, stick in a sprig of mint and serve at once.

- You can get a head start by putting the first batch, without mint, in the freezer.

- To frost: Grasp the rim of the filled cup with your fingertips and rapidly twist the cup back and forth until the outside is covered with heavy frost. Or churn with a spoon. Don't try this while drinking juleps yourself.

*I love that Sangria Wine—Love to drink it with old friends of mine.
Yeah I love to get drunk with friends of mine—When we're drinking
that old Sangria Wine.*

Jerry Jeff Walker, "Sangria Wine"

# sangria

This recipe was created and enjoyed by the best group of
Texans a man can know.

1 liter red wine

1 1/2 cups Brandy*

1/2 cup Triple Sec

1/4 cup simple syrup

2 apples, cut into bite-size cubes

2 pears, cut similarly

1 orange, sliced into a thin round

Club soda to taste

Combine the ingredients. Refrigerate at least 2–4 hours, or up
to 24 hours. Serve over ice. This recipe serves 6–8 thirsty folks.

*As with most mixed drinks, the amount of liquor you use
depends entirely on taste and preference (and, let's face it,
how often you drink . . .). For instance, the Texas version calls
for an addition of Jack Daniels (lots of it).

# miscellaneous
# party tips

## beauty doesn't have to fade
## (so fast)

Whatever flowers you choose to use to decorate the space in which you're entertaining—if you choose to use any at all—is entirely up to you. Most cut foliage can make a striking arrangement—tree branches, lilacs, peonies or roses. But by employing a few simple techniques, your floral décor can look better during the party and after.

Buy the flowers a day or two ahead of time so that they open nicely for your party.

When you get them home, immediately do the following:

- Fill the sink with warm water.
- Put the flower stems in that water.
- Find your vase(s).
- Drop some flower preservative in each vase.
- Put warm water in the vase.

- Cut the stems on an angle (this is so the flower can absorb water more readily).
- Arrange the flowers in your vase.

The day of the party, you can re-cut the flowers if they're not looking their best.

Ron and Sandie's tulip tip: put a penny in your tulip vase to perk up droopy flowers.

# reality check

### a rose by any other name . . .

is of course still a rose, and there is no substitute. Here's how to ensure that they look their best.

- Strip most leaves and thorns from the stems.
- Soak stems in the sink or in a bucket of hot tap water until it cools.

- Cut stems at an acute angle, using a sharp knife or scissors.
- Add a floral preservative.
- Remove the two outermost petals if you need the flower to open quickly.
- Pack the flowers into a vase (filled with water and preservative).

# flowers by season

The most affordable way to decorate your home with flowers is to choose flowers in season. Obviously, if you've got a garden, just use what you've got that looks good. But if you're buying, buy stems that are in season and save yourself some money and hassle (there's nothing worse than trying to find sunflowers in the winter in Connecticut). The following is a very general chart. Where you live plays a huge part in this, so check locally; those of you in Florida and California have better year-round selections than most of us.

| Winter | Spring | Summer | Fall |
|--------|--------|--------|------|
| Evergreens | Cherry blossoms | Aster | Amaryllis |
| Berries | Daffodil | Begonia | Autumn foliage |
| Forced bulbs | Dogwood trees | Black-Eyed Susan | Chrysanthemum |
| Poinsettia | Forsythia | Clematis | Coreopsis |
| | Hyacinth | Delphinium | Crab Apple |
| | Lilac | Gardenia | Dahlia |
| | Magnolia | Hydrangea | Gerber Daisy |
| | Peony | Poppy | Hydrangea |
| | Rose | Rose | Rose |
| | Tulip | Sunflower | Sunflower |

# your party is alive . . .
## with the sound of music

With very little thought, music can set a relaxing, welcoming ambience, start conversations, or make people get up and boogie. Whatever your desired result, here's a list of our favorite party albums

| Mellow Music Good Background Sounds | Music with a Bit More "Soul" | For the Dancing Queen in All of Us |
|---|---|---|
| Antonio Carlos Jobim *Songbook* | BB King *Anthology* | Abba *Gold: Greatest Hits* |
| Buena Vista Social Club *Buena Vista Social Club* | Bob Marley and the Wailers *Legend* | Aretha Franklin *Greatest Hits* |
| Edith Piaf *30th Anniversaire CD Set* | Etta James *Her Best: The Chess 50th Anniversary Collection* | Barry White *The Icon Is Love* |
| Erykah Badu *Baduism* | Johnny Cash *The Man in Black—Greatest Hits* | Chuck Berry *The Anthology* |
| Frank Sinatra *The Best of the Capital Years* | Lauryn Hill *The Miseducation of Lauryn Hill* | George Michael *Faith* |
| Keb' Mo' *Just Like You* | Paul Simon *The Rhythm of the Saints* | Hitsville USA: *The Motown Singles Collection* |
| Ottmar Liebert *Luna Negra* | Robert Earl Keen *Picnic* | Macy Gray *On How Life Is* |
| Verve Compact Jazz *Ella Fitzgerald & Louis Armstrong* | Willie Nelson *The Very Best of Willie* | Rockin Dopsie & the Zydeco Twisters *Louisiana Music* |

# "did I tell you all about the time when Jack and I and this stripper . . ." (toasts)

You may never have to give a toast. But you probably will, so please take a word from those of us who have heard hundreds of them, given a few, and have learned more than a few lessons. First things first: make it as brief as possible, and speak appropriately.

> One best man we know of gave a twenty-minute wedding toast that involved making the mother-of-the-groom do a Tequila shot, giving the groom a surfboard as a wedding gift, and stepping on the bride's veil, ripping it out of her hairdo.

If you're scripting a toast, remember that humor is always welcome and memories can be nice to share, but think long and hard about whether or not either are appropriate for the occasion and the audience. If you find a story essential, remember that good stories can usually be told without a 30-minute set-up. Two words: punch line.

> Julie gave a toast at her brother's wedding in both Spanish and English—a thoughtful attempt at inclusion—that was, unfortunately, too long in one language (let alone said twice in two). Know when to cut it short!

If you're at a loss for something to say or asked to give an impromptu toast, simply say a few nice yet sincere words about the guest(s) of honor and wish them well. In a nutshell: say something nice (that you mean), say something appropriate to the event, and don't carry on.

# out! out! darn spot!

## cleaning tips

Before a party, how well you clean your home largely depends on how prepared you are and how much time you have (or how much help you have). If you've got the time and the inclination, go to town. Clean everything in sight. Many people choose to use a party as a reason for a "spring cleaning." If you can, great. By and large, however, a sparkling clean house isn't necessary. If your guests notice dust bunnies behind the couch, we say they aren't paying enough attention to the conversation.

If you run out of time and need to do a fast cleaning, get the bathrooms as clean as possible and well stocked, then dim the lights and light candles.

# cleaning up

You can choose to clean up after your last guest leaves and before you go to bed, or in the morning. It all depends on you and what you prefer. Julie generally can't sleep knowing there's a dirty dish somewhere so except for the largest parties, she cleans up before bed. Ron, on the other hand, likes to clean up the next day, and for the larger parties, he's the one up at dawn cleaning up the street. Whatever works for you.

Cleanup is a lot easier if you plan a little ahead of time. As we mentioned earlier, if you do these things before the party, you'll save a lot of time and aggravation in the end.

- Run and empty your dishwasher.
- Empty your trashcans and put clean bags in them.
- Clear off counter space for dirty dishes.

During the party, try your best to clean as you go. If you do even a little bit of cleaning or picking up as you cook and serve, you'll be better off at the end of the event.

Then, after your party, try to do the following (and try to make it fun). If you entertain as a couple, like we do, clean up together. It will make the cleanup pass much more quickly, and it can also be fun. Just wait until your last guest is safely gone, turn on some lively music, and start cleaning up.

- Have a trash container near your sink for scraping.
- Scrape dishes as you bring them in, then stack them in sorted piles (for dishwasher, for hand washing).
- Have a bucket or something similar filled with soapy water for dirty flatware.
- Load and run the dishwasher.
- Put all food items away.

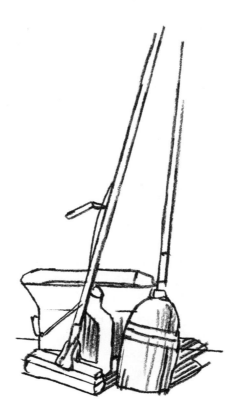

# how to be a good guest

We would be remiss to have gone on for so many pages about how to be a fabulous host if we didn't at least briefly mention how to behave graciously as a guest.

When you begin hosting parties more often (and it is our goal that you do), you will most likely begin receiving more invitations to others' parties. This is called reciprocation; when you've had someone to your home as a guest, they may, out of kindness, return the favor. Being a guest now and then is one of many blessings of hosting. First and foremost, you should act exactly as you would hope your guests would act.

## sixteen good guest tips

1 Respond to invitations in a timely, thoughtful manner.
2 Don't ask if you can bring an additional guest.
3 Don't even think about bringing anyone uninvited; this includes children.
4 If you offer help and the host declines, don't push the issue.
5 Dress appropriately.
6 Be prompt.

**7** If you wish to bring a hostess gift, bring something thoughtful and leave your expectations (of prominent display, or gushing, etc.) behind.

**8** Be as pleasant as possible. Be social. Mingle.

**9** Be complimentary (but sincere), and never criticize the host.

**10** If you make a mess or break something, apologize, try your best to fix it or clean it up (don't go overboard by scouring the house in search of a vacuum cleaner or superglue), then offer to pay for repairs or replacement.

**11** Don't talk on the cell phone or make phone calls or otherwise give the impression that you would rather be elsewhere.

**12** Don't drink too much and become a burden.

**13** Try not to leave early (even if the party's dreadful). If you must, have a good reason.

**14** Don't overstay your welcome. Check for cues from the host as to when you can make your leave. There's little question that if you're the last person there, and you're hanging out, drinking Port, rambling about taxes, it's time to go home.

**15** Gather all of your belongings when you do leave.

**16** Send a proper, handwritten thank-you note immediately after the party.

# be yourself

There is no better advice for us to give you than to tell you to please, be yourself. Too often, we listen to other people's "rules" and apply them to our own life, and this is both unnecessary and wrong. The people who set such rules or give advice (even us—with this book) don't know anything about your life, how you live it, or what makes you happy. Only you know yourself.

*We forfeit three quarters of ourselves in order to be like other people.*

Arthur Schopenhauer

Forget about anyone's "dos and don'ts." If you want to use Easter eggs as your centerpiece at Thanksgiving, well, go for it—if it makes you happy. If someone says that pastels are "in" and you dislike pastels, you shouldn't paint your dining room pink just because some "expert" thinks you should. Let your own sense of beauty guide you.

*It is an absolute perfection to know how to get the very most out of one's individuality.*

Michel de Montaigne

Be yourself. And share some of yourself with others. Spread the joy! Entertain! Throw a party, have some people over for drinks, organize a picnic.

Carpe Diem! Seize the day. After all, this is your life—and as our friend Sandy says, "it isn't a dress rehearsal."

Live it. Share it. Enjoy it.

*Let us endeavor so to live that when we come to die, even the undertaker will be sorry.*

Mark Twain

*What a wonderful life I've had! I only wish I'd realized it sooner.*

Colette

# bibliography

Baldrige, Letitia. *In the Kennedy Style: Magical Evenings in the Kennedy White House*. New York: Doubleday, 1998.

Poister, John J. *The New American Bartender's Guide*. New York: Signet, 1999.

*Webster's Universal College Dictionary*. New York: Gramercy Books, 1997.

**Throw a party! Enjoy!**

# index